The Next Step
with Spirit

THE NEXT STEP WITH SPIRIT

Extraordinary Events That Happen to ORDINARY PEOPLE

Charles Sommer

 DEVORSS *Publications*

ISBN: 0-87516-684-9

Library of Congress Catalog Card Number: 95-70038

DeVorss & Company, *Publisher*
Box 550
Marina del Rey, CA 90294

Printed in the United States of America

Dedication

I dedicate this book as a memorial to the loving memory of my mother, Lucy J. Sommer. She is more than a Mom, she is an eternal friend whose love and support will always be remembered. I love you forever.

Charles

Contents

Prelude

If your world was opened up through experiences like reading *The Celestine Prophecy*, *Saved by the Light*, or *Embraced by the Light*, it is time for you to take **The Next Step with Spirit**. Discover the extraordinary nonfictional events that are happening through ordinary people.

Each variety of extraordinary events uncloaks some of the mystery to Divine Guidance. We do not need near-death experiences to bring us into recognition of an internal and external guidance system in our daily lives. In an age when science is saying we cannot separate the observer from the thing observed, ordinary people are knowing we are not separated from our Source. We can really get "in-tu-it." "In-tu-it" is the root word for intuition. Intuition is the vehicle we use to access the infinite love and boundless intelligence I call Spirit.

In the early 70's, having participated in some life-changing seminars, an extraordinary thing happened. My intuitive facilities had the channel suddenly open wider by a burst of involuntary tears. Driving down the freeway one afternoon, tears just rolled down my cheeks. A huge emotional block I did not know existed had just melted away. A strong urge came over me to see my estranged brother. When my wife and I arrived at his house three hours later, my brother, René, greeted us at the curb. He wondered why I had called and set up this unexpected meeting.

We went inside his home and I explained to him and his wife what had happened to me on the freeway. ''I needed to see you, René, and let you know that I love you. I am giving up all my self-righteous judgments about you. Now I know my twenty years of condemning you created an emotional block to my ability to feel.'' I invited my brother to touch me, to feel the enormous rush of energy still moving through my body. His wife left the room. This awesome power expressing through me frightened her, while René seemed to appreciate my extraordinary aliveness. My spouse, Bobbe, thought I was acting very strangely.

My extraordinary aliveness carried over into my morning tennis match with a 21-year-old. This gentleman, Ron, had the speed of an angel along with excellent playing skills. In our three months of playing tennis together, this 40-year-old never won a match against him until this morning. My playing skills were enhanced by my unusual lightness and the ease with which I moved around the court. This lighter way of being splashed over into my business activities as well. I liked feeling this way.

Eventually my enlightened way of being in the world returned to normalcy. What had caused this spontaneous and extraordinary way of being in the world? What was it that returned me to a more ordinary way of living? I could never be the exact same person after this wonderful experience. I wanted to know more about this midlife transformation. I did something to trigger this extraordinary event. What was it? There was something more to life. What I had experienced I wanted to recreate. I wanted my brother to discover for himself what I had experienced. I offered to sponsor René into some of the self-awareness seminars that helped me gain insight into myself and others. René looked into some of them with me, signed up for one and backed out at the last moment. He was not ready.

Nineteen years later, as I am recording some of the extraordinary events that happen to ordinary people, I begin to grasp a deeper synchronicity that underlies the happening of the moment. I am compelled to share this book from conception to completion. The manuscript evolved in ways that give it a life of its own.

These short stories are intended to illustrate that there is a Divine Guidance system within the ordinary fabric we call Life. The value in taking the next step with Spirit is to penetrate the temporal rendition of life, to discover the resemblance of God as Spirit. Through the cultivation of our intuition we access Divine Guidance.

Taking the next step in harmony with Spirit requires understanding this: There is an ultimate reality, a beneficent Presence expressing Itself eternally everywhere as One Mind, One Life, One Expression.

There is a cure for spiritual Alzheimer's disease. We can produce the cure by getting "in-tu-it." Our extraordinary events are often light-years ahead of our ordinary understanding. It is through our intuitive faculties that the mysteries of life reveal themselves to us.

Each person's private experience of Divine Guidance is generously shared on the pages that follow. The explanations, admittedly, are expressed through a Judeo-Christian spiritual psychology which appreciates that anyone can get "in-tu-it" and take the next step with Spirit. As we open to It, It opens to us, for the observer and the observed are One in the Spirit.

As we synthesize our spirit with Spirit, we humbly accept the guidance of the Ultimate Conductor. We discover that our spiritual insights expressed become our glorious future. Doom and gloom give way to infinite love and boundless intelligence as we play in sync with Spirit.

In the year it took to write this book my brother, René, now sixty-five, went through an extraordinary change and really got "in-tu-it." You will recognize my brother in some of the short stories. Some of the stories may be difficult to believe. I suggest that you suspend your judgments. The stories are true and not drug-induced. Remember, what was once extraordinary is now ordinary.

As you really get "in-tu-it," enjoy *The Next Step with Spirit*.

An Acknowledgment

I would like to thank Jacqueline Neal, Carol Karpeck, Renee Surratt, Bobbe Sommer and Mary Hickey for their tremendous support in their frank editorial comments and grammatical corrections.

I do thank all the people who were so kind as to furnish us with accounts of their extraordinary events. They are:

Dawn Quiros	Juan Moreno
Nicole Christine	Jacqueline Neal
Paul Bura	Cousin Rose
Stella Horrocks	René Sommer
Carol Jenson	Doreen Fare
Lisa Jo Landsberg	Kay Michael
Mary Lou Hainer	Elaina Vaara
Hugh McVeigh	Eugene Maurey
Frances Adams Moore	V. Vernon Woolf
Margarita Felix	

I have a deep sense of gratitude to Arthur Vergara for discovering value in my writing and the willingness to publish it.

I thank God for guidance and for conducting the orchestration that has brought us all together, including those seen and unseen, known and unknown—individuals who have given this book a life of its own. May it bring a blessing to all that read it.

The Next Step

with Spirit

Introduction

As I awoke this morning what came to my mind was the metaphor and riddle "*What is the kernel of truth?*" The answer came swiftly: *The profound has to be in the ordinary.* The profound has to be in the mundane things, events, and happenings of life for us to discover and use.

Pro found: pro means "for" and *found* means "to find." The extraordinary is found in the ordinary. Ordinary people like us can gradually or suddenly unlock, unravel or trigger an awareness of the grand mysteries that lie hidden in the kernel of truth.

God knows the origin of the first kernel of wheat and the hidden attributes buried within its splendor. What did it take to discover that a kernel of wheat could be ground into flour? Who discovered flour could be mixed with water and baked to produce bread—enough to feed countless generations of humankind on planet earth? Just pause a moment and think how many varieties of bread exist. The first discovery of grinding wheat into flour opened the portal to greater discoveries. That is, if you consider rye, bran, or any of the twelve grains found in breads a greater discovery!

The mystery in the metaphor of the kernel of truth

resides in us, as us. It can't be any other way. Ordinary consciousness contains within it Superconsciousness. *We the ordinary people discover and use what Superconsciousness is providing.*

Superconsciousness is another label we give to Life. This Life Force or Spirit some of us call *God*. God is believed to be beyond all labels, boundaries or borders. Yet, within ourselves is the extraordinary awareness of the Divine Presence. The Divine Presence is often recognized as infinite Love, Light, Truth, Intelligence, Beauty, Power and the Source of all creativity. God as Source is the creative principle found in a kernel of wheat. In the kernel of wheat is Life Itself.

Let the Venture Begin

There are kernels of truth shared by individuals that may awaken a remembrance of the infinite power and presence of God. Venture into remembrance through the heart's desire to know God. There are some things the intellect remains blind to until the heart is open.

The first person who discovered the process of making bread from a kernel of wheat found the extraordinary in the ordinary shaft of wheat. The profound exists in the mundane.

What treasures are awakening through us now to meet the challenges of today? Just as the potential for bread lay dormant in the kernel of wheat for eons of time, what kernels of truth within us await our discovery?

Is there a way to call forth the extraordinary power within us? Do we dare to venture into the mystical union, into the frontier of eternity where Divine Guidance is not an option, but rather, Divine Guidance is a welcome choice?

Purpose

If we truly are sons and daughters of God, if our essential nature is Spirit, then what does it take for us to discover our God-like-ness? Can we become conscious of Divine Presence in every act, deed and activity? Is the very essence of God found in the ordinary and the extraordinary moments of life? In a book called *A Search for God*, by Edgar Cayce, it is written: *Through the activity of the will is the method by which each of us should prepare himself as a channel for forces that may assist in gaining a greater concept of the Oneness of the Father in the material plane.*

I started writing and gathering the material for this book a year ago, and I just realized it's about our willing and willful discovery that God exists in us as us. The appearances of separation vanish as we willingly and willfully seek the resemblance of God in all, as all. The extraordinary has always existed in the ordinary.

The purpose of this book is to share the extraordinary experience of a cross-section of ordinary people in today's world. *To touch somebody and move them toward enlightenment is a wonderful gift,* said actor Jack Lemmon during an interview on AMC's "Reflection of the Silver Screen" on

January 26, 1994. He observed that the mysteries of life are best explained by the arts.

Through the art of sharing some profound, intimate experiences of a wide circle of individuals, it is possible to sense an internal Divine Guidance system at work in our lives. We can learn to access, cultivate and use this extraordinary guidance system. Let the "silver screen" of our lives reflect what God wants. Let each of us, individually and collectively, honor through use the extraordinary power resident in us, as us.

Let the Divine Shine

The candlepower of a halogen or laser lamp is small compared to a God-centered glowing individual. An enlightened individual is a lamp of white light. Within the white light is the mind of God expressing Itself as the individual. It is ourselves in concert with the harmonic thoughts of an all-pervasive Super-self. What we once deemed extraordinary, indeed, has become ordinary to the spiritually aware person. *By spiritually aware I mean: people from any culture, ethnic background, religious, economic or political systems who are aware of Divine Presence, which animates all creation . . . including themselves.*

Let us choose Spirit as a reference, and let God's intuitive guidance system take us into a new frontier of knowing. This happened to Lisa Jo, a Boulder training consultant. Something guided her from financial disaster. Her experience, and the experiences of many others, can stimulate your Divine Guidance awareness. Divine Guidance is the obvious proactive choice for students of Truth.

Proactive means we are actively encouraging it to happen. By choice, we place our faith and interest in Divine Guidance and draw It to our awareness. Can this really be done? Yes. *For as many as are led by the Spirit of God, they are the sons [children] of God.* (Romans 8:14). Read on and discover how It works.

PART I

DIVINE GUIDANCE: A PROACTIVE CHOICE

A Boulder, Colorado, Training Consultant

Lisa Jo Landsberg describes how the guidance process worked for her:

Last Fall I finally found a townhouse I thought had all the features I wanted. The townhouse was in the final building stages and I was eager to find out how to purchase it. I tracked down the financial backer of the project and was given the opportunity to buy the townhouse I wanted, pending the successful outcome of escrow.

As a first-time buyer I relied on the help of a friend and expert to help me buy my first dream home. From all appearances, everything was going well for the completion of the purchase. However, my gut instinct kept bringing home the message that something was wrong. My gut instinct kept telling me to back out but I misread the message as fear of commitment for a first-time home buyer. I stayed in escrow until something extraordinary happened.

One night just before the final loan arrangement came though, I was watching the news on TV about the California fires. I had a thought about the townhouse and wondered what would happen to it if a fire occurred in the neighborhood. Would it burn? Would it be OK? Then something quite unusual happened. I had an intense feeling of heat in my body. I had a vision of the townhouse burning, not on my TV set but in the privacy of my mind. A strong sensation now accompanied this inner viewing. It is really taking place in my mind's eye and in my feeling nature. This experience is much more than day-dreaming. I almost felt sick to my stomach seeing my home-to-be burning out of control.

This sensation of devastating loss lasted maybe fifteen seconds. Within fifteen minutes, on my real TV set, a newscaster preempted the program I was watching. He announced that a fire was out of control in Boulder, which is where I live. He did not give the exact locations —details were to follow. I said aloud to the TV set, "*I know where the fire is.*"

Minutes later, the newscaster confirmed the location of the fire. My townhouse was burning to the ground. I guess my angels really didn't want me to make a bad investment.

Lisa Jo is a teacher of a popular Hatha Yoga class. Hatha Yoga is developed from an ancient Hindu wisdom —a philosophy which teaches us to unify self with Supreme-Self. This is the wisdom in the Ten Commandments, the Way of the Tao, the Eightfold Path and Christlike Love. Each of us needs to get more in tune with Spirit. It is Spirit that guides us in extraordinary ways. Yoga is a practice which teaches us to look within and to become still, something most of us fail to do in our hectic choice of lifestyles. Lisa understands the value of quiet prayer and meditation—that it brings a sense of expanded awareness into our ordinary lives.

Even the writers of the U.S. Constitution knew that humanity is created equal. Not equal in appearance or talents, but equal in Spirit. Since we value our diversity, then it is of paramount importance to cherish God in essence, to get involved in the activity of Spirit. Spirit lights the way, provides protection and guidance as we take the next step with Spirit.

United in Essence

Our souls, our spirits are interconnected in the fabric of the Almighty where Love/Intelligence/Law reside. Guidance is always right where we are. I use many examples of my own growing spiritual awareness as well as examples from a wide cross-section of humanity. Lisa Jo and many others were kind enough to give us their impressions of how Divine Guidance works for them. None of us has exclusive access to intuitive knowing. How we use, interpret and process information depends on our level of interest and our willingness to experience Life.

Discover for yourself, through the magic of real life in a series of human adventures, how God works. Let us learn to find our divine potential—learn the different methods, discover ways of awakening to what God wants to happen through us. All of us can in our own way develop and use our God-given talents. No one can do it for us.

When a young bird is ready to fly for the first time, it will leap out of the nest. Instinctively the bird knows how to fly. Like the bird, we intuitively know our purpose for being here. To grow dynamically into our purpose, we must seek the answers that are spiritually relevant for us. We are encouraged by others who have learned to co-operate with the guidance process. We can learn to soar with the spiritual eagles and nest in the higher under-standing of what God is.

Now is the holy instant we can tap into Universal Mind. As spiritual beings, we are required to bring into remembrance our God-likeness, and to take the next step with Spirit.

A Little Humor

A minister who knows well the intrinsic value in "right thinking" told me this cute story:

> There was an older lady in my congregation called Betsy. I went up to Betsy and told her, "You really must spend more time thinking about the hereafter, Betsy."
>
> Betsy curtly replied, "My dear Minister, I want you to know that I spend a great deal of time thinking about the hereafter. Every time I walk into a room I say to my-self, 'What am I here after?' "

The Key to Spiritual Awareness

A word of suggestion: as you read further, suspend your judgments on the contents. The stories are all nonfiction and come from ordinary people. My intent in sharing this private material is to enhance your spiritual awareness. There is an indescribable power for Good in the universe that you can use; and it can use you. The portal is through the renewing of the mind by consciously expressing the Will-to-Good. Spirit is more animated through us in extraordinary ways as we learn to identify with it, as Lisa Jo and others are doing. I encourage you, then, to start each day by becoming still as you access the Spirit within for 10 to 20 minutes.

Twenty-First-Century Citizen

We are better equipped to deal with change coming from our spiritual center. The twenty-first-century citizen, constantly confronted with enormity, magnitude and acceleration of change, needs to develop inner knowing. Change is happening. Everywhere, changes in lifestyles, jobs, professions and values are occurring. No person, family, institution, business or political system is immune to the spiritual acceleration happening today.

There is one constant, one center that perpetuates all changes, all recycling, all rebirth, all beginnings and all ends. That constant provides the Life Force, the etheric vitality. Within the Life Force is contained the inspiration, the motivation and solutions. As change happens, we are guided to express life as Its wonderful instrument. How does the Life Force work?

Life Force

The Life Force is not bound by precedent. The creative impulse is evident everywhere. Let's compare our process of Divine Unfoldment with the growth of a plant from seed to flower. The Life Force is the creative impulse in the seed, plant and flower. The seed requires the right quantity of good soil, water, air and sun, which are also activities of the Life Force.

How does the Life Force work through you? Like the seed, you have the potential to grow and become what the Life Force intends for you. The ground of your being is Spirit, the water is the grace that flows out of your humanity. The air is the breath that awakens the seed of your intention. The sun is the power that draws you up to itself and fires up your enthusiasm and moves you from ordinary to extraordinary.

A small seed is never lost in the dark, quiet solitude of the soil. Something within the seed has the faith in the unfolding process of life. The seed is not afraid of the darkness. The seed is filled with Life Force and through quiet contemplation realizes its potential. Like the plant, it is in your moments of quiet contemplation that you enter more deeply into the mind of God.

The Mind of God

If there is only one Mind, the mind of God, how does it work? God expresses through us, as us. It is our destiny to express the will of God. The grand and glorious beings that we all are in potential are known to God the Father. The archetypal image that we are created in the image and likeness of God is absolute. This pure, unconditional archetypal image is impressed in God-the-Mother's womb. The Mother's womb is a metaphor for the creative medium in the mind of God. It is the feminine aspect of God that gives birth to creation. It is the sacred child waiting to be acknowledged. It is a divine idea that we can never abort; a grand and glorious being waiting to be recognized. The self is knowing the Self! It is we ordinary individuals seeking the extraordinary Presence we call Spirit.

Let us now unravel the mystery of how Spirit works through us as us. Remember, to get the most from these genuine accounts, it really helps to suspend judgment. Discover the diverse ways Spirit works through us, from the ordinary to the extraordinary aspects of itself.

Whether we know it or not, we are using the mind of God. It is truly helpful for us to become consciously aware of how Mind works. The extraordinary events that lead to our proactive use of Divine Mind are many. As we learn to cooperate with God, our success is assured. Here is an example of how Spirit works by invitation through Barbara Cartland.

The Most Successful Romantic Novelist

The English romantic novelist Barbara Cartland has written 600 novels, averaging one million copies sold; i.e. 600 million books to her credit. In her interview with

Inside Edition, which aired on cable television June 5, 1994, she reported the following: *I say a short prayer to God and soon my mind fills with the plot for the next novel.* This is one example of how an extraordinary event has become ordinary to Barbara. I would say this extraordinary lady used ordinary wisdom, the wisdom found in most religious traditions. What wisdom is that? The wisdom to seek guidance from an infinite Source. Barbara in a prayerful state becomes a receptive medium, an instrument of infinite Intelligence and boundless Love. As a writer, Barbara is keenly aware of God as an endless, omnipresent Source of guidance. As she surrenders to what God wants to express through her, her intuitive mind receives the direct impression and she fulfils her purpose by sharing with us her inspired works.

Barbara uses Divine Mind and Divine Mind uses Barbara to the extent that she is open and receptive to it. It does require her proactive choice to bring the material into physical expression as a manuscript. It does require prayerful solicitation and a prescribed use of Divine Mind. Also, it is unique that none of her romantic characterizations is sexually explicit. Also, no authors to my knowledge have exceeded or come close to her success, although most of her paragraphs contain three sentences or less.

Nuclear Medicine

Scientists also use the mind of God to create extraordinary tools to facilitate the healing process. A medical doctor, who is a tennis-playing friend, told me last week that nuclear medicine just saved his life. It saved him from bleeding to death internally and from exiting this expression of life.

I asked him, ''Doc, what happened to you?''

He replied, ''I was bleeding internally and it showed up in my stools when going to the toilet. Normal X-rays and CAT scans could not detect the source of bleeding. A nurse took a small amount of blood from my body, charged it with nuclear radiation, and redeposited into my blood stream.''

''Then what happened?'' I asked.

''The medical technician tracked my blood. We could see my blood running through my body on a highway resembling a tree. We detected charged blood running through my veins and arteries leaking out a side of my colon. Where the blood leaked, we could see it changed colors. The surgeon went in and removed the damaged part of the colon. I will be back playing tennis in a few weeks.''

Doc also told me that his father went into the hospital bleeding with the same problem forty-five years earlier and died in three weeks. Extraordinary methods restored Doc.

All extraordinary methods, inventions, art forms or talents come form one Universal Source who acts through us. If God is for one, then God is for all. The sun and stars shine on the just and the unjust. Perhaps in our minute view of the eternal, we are partially blinded to the law of cause and effect. What may seem fair or unfair in this moment of now is the eternal consequence of all our prior choices. God is helping us understand how Spirit works through us as us. Do we listen for guidance? Here is one who did:

Schoolteacher

A schoolteacher named Kay, with a son in the military, told me his unit had entered into a danger zone. She had deep concerns about his welfare. She prayed earnestly for his safety and asked a church group to pray for him also. Kay constantly worried and prayed. On the fifth day, as she was driving down the freeway, Kay received a message from God that she will never forget.

I asked Kay, "What was the message and how did you get it?"

She said, "The message was, *Are you going to stop worrying and let me run things?* The message came as bold thoughts which formed into the words of a sentence and appeared on a chalkboard in my mind." Could you tell from her statement that Kay taught English?

God wants our eyes inwardly focused, but not on worrying. We are constantly bombarded with masses of information unequaled in the known history of Planet Earth. Spiritually aware individuals are drawing out of Superconscious mind all that is required to make intelligent, loving, inspired choices.

In fulfilling our purpose for being here, we often have a sense of guidance and protection. The twenty-first-century citizen chooses what the subconscious mind already knows. What is that? God has given us all that we require to develop our spiritual abilities. Spiritual power comes through the Will-to-Good. This becomes more evident to me in my desire to bridge the gap to the eternal.

The next story is from a teenage boy who made an extraordinary decision that greatly enhanced his capacity to become what Spirit expected of him.

Paul, a Retired Canadian Engineer

Paul as a young boy learned early in life the benefit of honoring the Spirit within. This is his interesting story:

> My family lived in the western Ukraine, which before the second World War was a part of Poland. It was occupied in September 1939 by the Soviet Red Army. My father, who was a member of Polish Parliament, representing the Ukrainian minority, was arrested and sent to a slave labor camp. My mother and I were deported to Siberia, where we were allowed to lead "normal" lives confined to our little town. My mother, who was a skilled tailor, could earn enough money to send me to school. I was fourteen years old.
>
> After Germany's attack on the Soviet Union, Polish citizens, released from the slave labor camps, joined the Polish army to fight the Germans. The Polish army formed in Central Asia, thousands of miles from where my mother and I lived. My father was released from the slave labor camp and allowed to join us in Siberia. We were not Polish and had no interest in joining the army.

For a few months, despite hardships, we had a renewed family life.

Then suddenly while at school one day something illogically happened through my ordinary mind. I got a strange, strong, feeling, and a powerful thought that I will never forget. This strange thought was to join the Polish army in Central Asia. I got a feeling of absolute necessity: *I must go now and join the army.* I was only sixteen. My parents were stunned, yet strangely did not try to stop me. The next day, without money or food, I got on the train. Two days later, I joined the Polish army.

Of course, it proved to be the right decision. It took me from a brutal police state to the West and opened possibilities that had not consciously occurred to a young boy of sixteen or his parents. This inner, spiritual guidance sees with an all-seeing eye. To me this was an intervention of karma or Divine Providence/Guidance. It does not matter what we call it. For me, it is an unshakable proof that there is a meaning and purpose in our lives and help in its fulfillment.

At any age, we can develop an uncommon sense that guides and leads us through troubled, turbulent changes. God's presence is always with us, as us. The proactive choice is to recognize what God wants. Do we feel guidance?

Thank you, Paul Bura, Doctor of Science, for sharing your insights on how Spirit works through you. The next event comes from England. Prayer results in a meaningful vision.

Doreen, an English Nurse

Doreen Fare, a charming lady from Bristol, England, shares her experience this way:

> Often during my life I have been aware of "unseen" help, but the most memorable time was as follows: In my mid-forties, I worked as a nurse in a geriatric hospital, having previously held secretarial positions in my younger years. Now I was divorced and middle-aged, and had three teenage daughters and a young son of six to support.
>
> Spiritually, I believed I was learning the lesson of humility as I was only auxiliary nursing, and youngsters who could have been my daughters were in nursing charge. However it was my opinion that many of them should not be wearing a nurse's uniform. They were irritable and occasionally extremely unkind toward their patients. After observing this sad situation, I held the whole problem in my constant prayers. The meditation group I was leading was asked to direct light—large circles of light—and love to the very earth the hospital stood upon and to all around the hospital. The situation appeared to worsen and the unkind nurses appeared to direct their animosity mainly toward me. Every morning I asked God to protect, guide, and strengthen me before I went into work and thankfully returned each evening.
>
> One evening, I found my bicycle tires completely flat and the rain pouring down. I started my long three-mile walk home. There were no buses that went in that direction. I prayed that God would give me the strength and the energy to get home to the children after ten hours of heavy-duty nursing.

Suddenly I had a vision! A very beautiful angelic being showed herself to me in a cloud of silver and pale
blue. Her beautiful, serene, and shining face looked into
mine, and with thought-transference she said, "Your
prayers have been heard: my mantle of protection is all
around the hospital." When the vision faded, I found
myself very near my home, and I felt refreshed and up-
lifted. No tiredness.

A few weeks after this vision, as I went on duty there
was much talk among my nursing colleagues, who were
saying, "Isn't it strange! Many nurses are leaving."
Most amazing, all those leaving were the unkind ones.
Even more amazing: soon afterwards I remarried and,
a few years later, my new husband was asked to give lec-
tures upon healing in this hospital. I noticed that the
hospital had a very happy air about it.

Thank you, Doreen. It is no accident. Currently there
are many people experiencing angelic beings in visions.

Divine Plan

The meaning conveyed by these experiences is important
to the individual seeker of Truth, and it is equally important to those of us who are collectively interested in
spiritual awareness. Although I see through the eyes of
a student and teacher of Christian Mysticism, I marvel
at the cosmic forces plentifully at work. It is most apparent to me, extraordinary events come about through the
extraordinary use of our ordinary minds—our ordinary
minds working in collaboration with the Divine Plan.

God's power is right where we are. The challenge is how to discover and use the power in a beneficial way.

The Uncommon Sense

Let us not discuss the ordinary senses of sight, hearing, smell, taste or touch. Let us go immediately to a perception of power greater than we are, that we are one with in Spirit. *Webster's New Collegiate Dictionary* gives us a hint of how the uncommon sense works:

> **sense** (a) capacity for effective application of powers of the mind as a basis for action or response; intelligence.
> (b) . . . agreement with or satisfaction of such power.

Innate Intelligence is expressing within us. Our job is to discover the vital Force. To take Its guidance seriously, we must bring ourselves in concert with absolute, unconditional love. True love brings complete satisfaction and an uncommon sense of peace.

As a citizen of the twenty-first century, we can develop a keener sense of the power of God expressing Itself through us. Our capacity for effective application of powers of the mind as a basis for action or response depends on our interest. We may ask ourselves, *Are we interested in coming into agreement with the underlying unity of all?* If we are, how can we know when our small minds are attuned to Spirit? How do we know our actions are in Divine accord? The answer is simple: check our level of satisfaction. Do we feel an uncommon sense of peace in the face of conflict?

A basis for action or response comes from a sense of complete satisfaction. That satisfaction comes from an inner knowing. Knowing what? Knowing the mind we use is the mind of God. When our mind agrees with what God wants, bliss or its complement is sure to follow. Extraordinary events are complementary and a necessary outcome to where we place our interest.

My Wife, the Centerfold

Nearly four decades ago, I placed some of my interest in an attractive, active blond college student who still amazes me. Her name is Bobbe, my then wife-to-be. We met at the University of Colorado.

A sense of adventure drew me to the University of Colorado. I had never been to Colorado. No member of my family had ever gone to college. Too much of my life tempo was offbeat, struggling to find my identity in the confines of my limited belief system. My tempo was a heartbeat away, living in the shadow of my potential rhythm.

What drew me to Bobbe was the melody of an upbeat tempo rhythmically expressing through her. This unseen rhythm was evidence of her exuding confidence from a deep inner knowing. The white light, radiating from her eyes, sparkled a vibrance that was enchanting. An upbeat rhythm and radiance indicated an attunement with her purpose for being. On the downbeat Spirit expresses It-self through her form. (I liked her shapely form as well.) She did not try to be something she is not.

What drew me to Bobbe like a magnet was her determination, her compassion, her selfless sense of service. Her desire to go beyond the confines of society that would keep women in their traditional place waxed strong. Perhaps she was drawn to me because something in her knew that I would support her in being the radiant person she is. There is no last frontier or limitation to Spirit. We truly help one another evolve into our higher potential as we lift our self out of the bog of the ordinary. Our individual self, resonating as spirit, moves us to the upbeat of Spirit. New awareness comes into our experience on the downbeat, into our individual selves from the Divine Orchestrator. This is the Divine Composition of the creative Force at work, in us as us.

On the eve of our thirty-seventh wedding anniversary, she became the centerfold, the pin-up of success in the June 1994 issue of *Entrepreneur* magazine. A full-page color picture of her in the center of the magazine was followed by an interview entitled, ''Think Positive,'' subtitled, ''Yes, You Can Program Yourself for Success,'' by Robert McGarvey. It is a well-written article on the value and use of Mind. The article emphasizes that we need to change our belief system. Magical forms of thinking believe that it will be given *to* us, rather than *through* us. What we give our interest to makes a difference in what comes up in our experience. The real science in thinking is putting our mind to work in an intuitive, disciplined focus. Success is sure to follow as we correctly interpret our Divine Guidance.

As I write, it is our thirty-seventh wedding anniversary. My spouse had wanted me to join her in New York on this day, where she had gone to join her colleagues and promote their new manuscript into a book. The manuscript addresses the particular problems women encounter in climbing the corporate ladder. A noble cause, a creative impulse, motivated them to go to New York. After wrestling with my compulsive need to please Bobbe, I decided not to join her. She was honoring her impulse. Her satisfaction grows out of her creative expression. I felt my right place was working on this manuscript. She understood. I left word on her voice mail (which seems so impersonal, yet is an efficient way to reach her on this special day) this message: "I love you and will be with you in spirit. And aren't you glad that you can't hear my spirit snore?"

Personal Example

In the mid-70's I was a family man participating in many activities such as camping, Little League baseball, tennis, skiing, professional sales assocation and insurance marketing. Many early mornings before my shower and breakfast I would spread a towel out in front of the bedroom TV and do stretching exercises with Richard Hittleman. Hittleman's Hatha yoga program was a good way for me to start the day. His two attractive female helpers made the time pass pleasantly. The last five minutes of the program were spent on meditation, a subject I knew little about.

Two to three years into practicing Hatha yoga an extraordinary event happened through me. The event concerned a small tumor that I developed on my left hand between my thumb and my forefinger. This frightened me because I had a history of skin cancer—and now had a dime-size tumor under the skin. I knew the tumor would be undetectable in a physical exam unless I alerted the examining physician.

In the meantime, I decided to use the white light Hittleman called prana to eliminate the tumor. While in this slightly altered state of meditation, I would imagine white light dissolving the tumor. It reminded me of the times I poured bleach into the laundry water and the soiled white clothes minutes later came out spotless. Each day after the morning and evening healing treatment I could check the size of my tumor. If it were growing rapidly, I would have it surgically removed. In three days the tumor was gone. Was this coincidence or what?

What is this white light? Eric Butterworth says in his book *In the Flow of Life*, "Light is the reality of God within all creation." I guess God's white light is good for getting tumors out of our own physical garments.

Ordinary People

Who is ordinary? As people, we have similar biochemistry, physiology and biological urges that are ordinary. We all have the basic needs for human survival. Each of us is imbued with a faculty that gives us the opportunity to experience extraordinary events, events that trigger spiritual awareness. Extraordinary events are happening more frequently today and are definitely accelerating our awareness to new frontiers of the dynamics of Life.

The dictionary defines *extraordinary* as "that which is beyond what is usual, ordinary, regular, or established." The second definition is "exceptional in character, amounts, extent, degree, etc." Well, I have met the exceptional character of many ordinary persons around the world. I have asked these persons from diverse backgrounds to share with us some rare, divinely inspired events.

My motive is to examine what prompts these events in us. What is our part in providence? Can we conceive that Divine Guidance is open to all? As a seeker of Truth, I constantly need to surrender my parochial or narrow view of what is real and what is unreal. I need to suspend my judgments and beliefs to get to the core—a task sometimes very difficult, but possible.

Some extraordinary events seem unreal to us. They are beyond our ordinary understanding. What we don't understand is often written off as an illusion or something we don't talk about for fear of being labeled something undesirable. Yet God does persist at providing solutions to our heart's desire as happened with the carpet salesman.

The Carpet Salesman

My brother, René, a sixty-four-year-old carpet salesman, had experienced a deep, two-year recession in his business. He was struggling to keep the creditors away from putting him out of business. In the meanwhile, our eighty-one-year-old mother was gravely ill and literally staying alive to see him. René did not have the money to travel or the time to leave his failing business. René kept getting urgent calls from friends and relatives close to his mother saying that the time of her death was imminent. If he wished to see her, he must do it soon.

René had a keen interest in horse-racing. He could tell you more than you would care to know about horse races, jockeys and trainers. He got the idea that if he could make a winning by betting on the horse races he would visit his mother. With some $1,000 winnings, he would buy an airline ticket, rent a car, and stay in a motel while visiting his ill mother. Like a seed in his subconscious mind, this worthwhile idea went to work.

Not many days passed when René awoke one morning with a very strong feeling that gave him the impression that this was the day. This gut feeling generated within him a positive attitude, a stimulus prompting him to go to the gambling establishment. Once at the gambling establishment, he needed to draw upon all his experience, education, and intuitive knowing to have the odds of winning in his favor.

Most sophisticated gamblers are really conservative. They are very well informed, analytical and calculating.

Most professional gamblers avoid wild speculation. René fell into this sophisticated, well-informed gambling class. He even raised and bred a few racehorses of his own. In today's race, at one of the big California tracks, René knew the capabilities of three horses running in a field of 12 horses. He decided to ask God's help. René assured God that he would use his winnings to visit his mother whose desire to see him kept her alive. She also asked for God's help.

René decided to bet in an extremely risky manner, where the law of probability was beyond his ability to calculate the tremendous odds. René selected four horses in a twelve-horse race. Each horse had to finish the race in the exact order selected. He picked one horse to finish first, another to finish second, another to finish third and one to finish fourth. He felt good about the first three picks. The fourth horse he picked was a mystery. He had no conscious awareness of its ability. When the four horses crossed the finish line in the exact order that he picked them, he was quite excited. When they flashed the dollar pay-out on the screen, he was flabbergasted. And when he went to the window to claim the winnings on his $48 bet, he received net of over $9,000 after the 28% income tax deductions. René took his three sons to see his Mom. Grandma got an extra treat by having all four relatives visit her.

René said to me:

Charlie, I am not a religious person, but I know I had help. Just like the time I was making a sales call, and another extraordinary, embarrassing yet funny event happened. I was bending over showing some carpet samples to a homeowner when my bottom dentures fell out. The lady homeowner, with the swiftness of a cat, caught my dentures before they hit the floor. We both sat on the floor and laughed till tears ran down our cheeks. She said to me, "What do I do with your dentures?" I said, "I guess I'd better wash them."

I asked René if he made the sale. He said, "Yes. It broke the ice."

Ordinary Meditation

This next event was even stranger to my conservative mentality than the dissolving of a tumor through meditation. This event, which happens either to saints or to the mentally ill, happened to me, and I am neither. I knew of no one who had this or a similar experience. Again, I just completed my morning stretching exercises, ending with a brief relaxing body meditation. I got up from my towel that was lying on the floor in front of the TV. In my quiet master bedroom I sat on the edge of my bed in meditation. I mentally asked this question in the stillness of my mind: *What is the meaning of life?* Lo and behold I got an answer from an internal voice! This voice was distinct from a mental thought. It was a firm, yet gentle male voice that said, *Seek the resemblance of God.*

What is going on here? What does it mean to seek the resemblance of God? I shared the excitement of the moment with my wife who was preparing breakfast for the boys. For me, this experience was like breaking the sonic barrier to God or possibly one of His representatives. My wife, who seemed to take my news in her stride, kept fixing pancakes and said, "It is probably some part of your self." That was not a good enough answer to me. I decided to go to a higher authority. I consulted the dictionary.

> **re-semblance** . . . stemming from a French word, *resembler* (*re* + *sembler*) . . . to be like; in English 1 (a) correspondence in appearance. (b) a point of likeness

I knew what the words *seek* and *God* meant from childhood. Re-semblance: *re* means to return, go back to; *semblance* = the likeness of God.

I never read or heard anything expressed quite that way, even with my nine years of religious schooling as a child. My Bachelor of Science degree did not prepare me for an internal voice. I knew I was not crazy or imagining what happened. Well, fifteen years later I am much better prepared to hear that voice but it has not returned to my conscious awareness. Yet, I am more conscious than ever of an inherent flow of guidance in myself and in all creations. For me, internal guidance moved from a theoretical model into a practical reality.

Theo-centric

Theoretically, we all have a theory about God even if we are agnostic or atheist. Theology is the study of God and His relationship to the world. So theoretically and practically if God is everywhere, we need go nowhere to find God. Yet my inner voice said, *Seek the resemblance of God.* That resemblance is Spirit. Spirit is Love. This is a simple answer. Love has no boundaries, has no legal limits or human constraints. Love cannot be measured or metered out. Love cannot be confined to dogma, doctrine or ideology. There are many good books on what Love is, including the book I wrote with lots of help, called *The Dynamics of Living Love.* Theo-centric is having God as the central interest and ultimate concern. The internal God and the external are One and the same. Someone once wrote, "God is at the center and circumference of all things." "To know God is to know God in Spirit and Truth." What does that mean?

This is why the word *resemblance* is so important in my internal message. What is truth to you? What is Love? All I know is there is a law of attraction. What we give our attention to increases our awareness. Our awareness of love expands as we delve more deeply into its mystery. Love translates itself into meaningful activity. Just as a bird is guided into a warmer climate or a seed into a plant, we become more conscious of that which we seek.

What is satisfying and blissful to our soul is rendering to God what is God's. This means to use the gifts given

us in selfless service. There is no greater gift to give than
love.

Young Waitress

Yesterday, in a local restaurant, a young lady mistakenly
brought me a beef taco instead of the fish taco I had or-
dered. As I took my first big bite she informed me of her
mistake. She quickly made an exchange. It did not bother
me or the owner-chef of the place that the waitress made
a mistake. Later, as I was paying the bill to the young table server, she commented, "I've got a headache. It must
be from something I drank this morning." I told her, "I
have helped many people get rid of headaches by a brief
massage to the neck. Would you like to get rid of yours?"

As she sat in the chair, I took my left hand and held
her chin. With my right hand, I massaged some very
tight blood vessels in the side of her neck as I silently
asked God for help. I informed her that I could feel the
blood vessels relax and the flow of blood was now unobstructed to the brain. She informed me that the headache
was gone. I assured her this was more than the power of
suggestion. What she drank did not give her a headache.
It is what she told herself. Her inner critical child created
tension that resulted in a headache.

How many of us can forgive ourself or others for making some mistakes? Love heals wounds. That is my reality. She could have avoided the headache if she did not

take herself too seriously. *Let not your heart be troubled, neither let it be afraid* (John 14:27). If she were only more aware that her negative internal talk was creating her undesirable experience! The critical, negative tones of thought produce our experiences of headache, sore back, tight neck, etc.

At that day ye shall know that I am in my Father, and ye in me, and I in you (John 14:20). Yes, there is an inner spiritual unity that pervades the outer diversity. The outer diversity is like an infinite scale called *macrocosm* and *microcosm*. There is no end to big or little universes. No matter how much we delve into outer and inner space, there is ceaseless more. Yet within the endless fabric there is a harmonic resonance, a Divine melody that permeates all creation. Everyone and everything is imbued, guided and directed by a Universal Orchestrator that pulsates as the upbeats into the macrocosm and the downbeats into the microcosm of Divine Mind. Our *offbeat* is the sin of not being in attunement. At times we are expressing off key. There is always a solution for finding and using the right key or keys.

Principle and Presence

The keys to the Executive Suite of Spiritual Awareness are complementary. However, keys are of no use unless we use them. The complementary keys are called: Principle and Presence. What are these complemental keys and how do we use them? Love is a Principle and a Presence. In other words, the headache that the waitress had is a call to Love.

I wrote a good book called *Licking Your Wounds* on this subject. Am I an expert on the subject? No! I am a student, teacher, and writer on the subject of Truth. Many students of Truth have discovered it is necessary to transform the mind to achieve a modicum of inner Peace in our quick-changing, turbulent world.

I capitalized Peace because I understand it is our God-given potential. It is the resonant tune in the Chief Executive suite. It is the melody to seek and to find within ourselves. It is a quality of Spirit attainable by all. Peace is a Principle and a Presence. Can we know and express an attribute of God such as Peace? Yes.

Can the above waitress "chill out" or, as the English put it, "not to worry"? Yes. The golden key is awareness. Self-awareness comes in many forms—physical, emotional, mental. The most important of all is spiritual awareness. Can we redeem our spiritual awareness? *Yes.*

Redeem Spiritual Awareness

Redemption is spiritual awareness brought through us, as us. The holy instant is full of Peace. Headaches abide in the shadow of Peace. Peace is not necessarily something you get at death. Peace of mind is available to the waitress, to me, and to you always. Attaining, maintaining and sustaining a sense of Peace in the physical, emotional and mental bodies depends on Spiritual awareness.

Redemption is not something imposed on someone by the Almighty. We have free will to seek it. Redemption is a product of involution, a divine remembrance. Jesus, Buddha, Krishna, Zoroaster, and Muhammad knew the presence of God to be an enlightened comforter, a holy paraclete (Holy Spirit's aid or support), an inner teacher bringing all things to remembrance. It is a process of Spiritual development. No one religion, philosophy, science or political system has a lock on Truth. Truth is a Principle and a Presence like unto Peace. Just as a particle and a wave can't be separated, Peace and Truth can't be separated. One has the elusive properties and qualities of the other.

Proactive Spiritual Awareness

How we use our mind is important to our well-being. For instance, we use our intellect to process data that seems logical, rational and linear. Another aspect of our mind is the emotional investment in ideas, beliefs, pictures, people, events and things. We store emotions in some form of memory/body/mind. Science is currently discovering the whole is in the part. Mystics have known it for ages. *At that day ye shall know I am in my Father, and ye in me, and I in you* (John 14:20).

What does rule our mind? If our mind is ruled by our

intellect, we have a cold, calculating, exacting personality. If our mind is ruled by our emotional body, we have a reactive personality. If we use our creative mind to develop our *infundibulum* (not to worry; I will explain later), our personalities are proactive; we are a beneficial presence unto the world. The exacting and reactive personalities look for security in the world. The proactive personality is a seeker of Truth. Where is Truth? The answer is simple. Truth is in the whole and the part. How can Truth be accessed? Let us examine *infundibulum* for a clue.

Infundibulum

Infundibulum is a precious word given to my wife and me by the very wise, fun-loving 101-year-old Archbishop Warren Watters. My very talented and beautiful wife, Bobbe, asked Archbishop Warren, "How do you think I can best impart to my readers how to achieve the happiness habit?" The magical word he gave us was *infundibulum*. Our ignorance of the word was obvious. He directed us to use his extensive library in the same room where we were having our discussion. Bobbe quickly looked up the word and read it aloud to us.

> **infundibulum** 1: the hollow conical process of gray matter to which the pituitary body is continuous with the brain. 2: funnel.

We asked this extraordinary man: if the secret of his happiness was a "funnel," what did funnel mean to him? How did he use his funnel? "Please explain?" With a twinkle in his eye and a smile on his face, he readily elaborated the following:

> Every day I meditate on happiness. I see the great universe funneling through the top of my head and throughout my being. Here, in my mental/emotional/ spiritual infundibulum, I let it all pass through me and I accept everyone and everything as being in its right and proper place. My infundibulum allows me to funnel the spiritual into the material until they blend into one. When it's working, I can *think with my heart and hear with my head.*

Thank you, Warren, that is a golden tool and a wonderful idea to cultivate happiness. Joy is a Divine attribute that is not just approachable but is attainable by all who seek it. Humankind is evolving from emotional and/or intellectual dominance to a proactive choice to *think with our hearts and hear with our heads.* We will examine heart qualities later. But let us take a peek into the evolution of human consciousness.

Evolution of Human Consciousness

The evolution of human consciousness is growing. The observer and the observed are in a cosmic dance of in-

finite proportions. Stay with me now as we take a jour-
ney to explore the dynamics that cause extraordinary
events because of an internal/external force I call God.
If you are nonreligious, or think you are nonreligious,
feel free to call this eternal power by any name you wish.
Some of us call it Life Force, Mind, Allah, Hu, Christ,
Father or Mother Nature. Some of us say it has no name.
It is Indescribable.

The important idea is to recognize the One Power that
animates all things as universally present. To funnel the
Divine attributes through us is a proactive choice. Some
choices are made before this incarnation, before our
showing up in this body form. Illumination is a proactive
choice. It is a path of Self-discovery.

Historically, we the people once believed that the world
was flat and, for that matter, solid. Many thousands of
years ago on this planet humankind consisted of hunters
and gatherers. They were instinctively driven like the
squirrel to gather nuts, or like the bird that flies to
warmer climates in the winter for self-preservation. Survival and reproduction were ruled more by the emotional
body, instinctive awareness, a gut feeling.

Then we went through thousands of years and developed more keenly the use of intellect. Ancient Egypt,
with its libraries and monuments, and Ancient Greece,
with its beautiful buildings, objects of art and philoso-
phies, lighted the way. Ancient India, with the enlightened path of the Buddha, and China with the illuminated
way of the Tao are inspired through a divine influx of infinite Intelligence. Moses with the Ten Laws and Jesus

through his countless examples are inviting us to choose first the gifts of the Spirit, and all else is then provided.

19th-Century Discovery

A nineteenth-century researcher, Richard Maurice Bucke, M.D., looked for the common ingredients in historically illumined individuals. Dr. Bucke's book *Cosmic Consciousness* gives us examples of some individuals who learned to funnel more purely the attributes of God. These men and women were called saints and sages, God-like, Christ-like, enlightened beings. Jesus did not declare Himself the divine exception. He declared Himself the divine example. "You too can do greater things than I, if you first turn to God within." Does this mean we can be greater than God? No. This means we too can express the attributes of the Almighty only to the extent we abide in Truth. That, too, is a proactive choice.

Intelligence

Intelligence is another attribute of God found everywhere. The artist, the inventor, the scientist, the farmer, the merchant, the engineer, the teacher, the parent, the child, etc.—all the kingdoms of the earth, the earth itself, the galaxies—are all imbued with the resonating vibration of the Eternal One. The point is, if we want more happiness, more love, more talents, we must develop our infundibulum. We must consciously funnel and invite these treasures of the Spirit into our experience in a way that works for us.

Involution is the name for direct access to intuition— direct knowing without knowing why we know. Human evolution is the result, the effect, the product of living what we know.

In his research Bucke discovered that some of the earliest writings, like Homer's *Iliad* and *Odyssey* and ancient sacred texts, only mention about three or four colors. Joseph's coat of many colors (Genesis 37:3) was made for him by his father, Jacob (later called Israel). This is significant because the colors were most likely various hues of a few basic colors. Human consciousness had not reached our expanded way of knowing.

Each one of us plays a vital part in bringing to awareness what already exists in Spirit. High technological potential always existed. We have expanded our color-awareness even to the invisible realm of infrareds and ultraviolets. Science and technology have made across-the-board giant-strides. What is our next step with Spirit? Are we ready to take an extraordinary step with Spirit?

We take the resource of advanced technology and use it with compassion to solve and resolve our global challenges of hunger, homelessness, disease, pollution and other environmental issues. Read the story of Joseph in Genesis and see how one intuitive person saved the Israelites and Egyptians from hunger. What is your intuition capable of doing for our global family?

What does it take for you, for me, to courageously live

our enlightened choice? Warren Watters says, *We must think with our heart and listen with our mind.* Joseph Campbell, well-known, brilliant teacher and author wrote: *We can learn to know and come to terms with the greater horizons of our own deeper and wiser, inward self* in his book *Myths to Live By.*

The Message and the Messenger Are One

Joseph, the boy with a coat of many colors, had many spiritual gifts. He later used these gifts beneficially for Egypt, for the Hebrew nation and even for his brothers who had sold him into slavery. Let us discuss his father, Jacob, who gave him the coat in the first place.

Jacob raised his spiritual consciousness. He knew he had wronged his brother out of his rightful inheritance and this troubled him until an event happened that opened his heart and he took decisive action to right the wrong. We can learn from his experience as told in the book of Genesis. Like most of us, it took Jacob a prompting for him to heal a troubled relationship.

This is our story of what is happening on an accelerated basis today, to many people. Jacob wrestled all night with his emotionally-driven thoughts of fear. His fear regarding his ill treatment of his brother Esau became tantamount. The injustice he caused his brother over a prolonged period got to him. He was ready to make amends. He asked God's help through prayer. Jacob made financial restitution through many gifts to his brother. God opened Jacob's heart, with his cooperation. Jacob had redeemed himself with his brother Esau and in the sight of God. Redemptive Love comes through the heart, and it rules the intellect and the emotions. Like Jacob, we too can learn to manage from the heart.

Four authors—H. Bracey, J. Rosenblum, A. Sanford and Roy Trueblood—wrote *Managing from the Heart*. It is easy to read. It is a book about current principles used in managing a business successfully. I'll identify these principles soon. They are good guides to living a harmonious, abundant, and joyful life. Perhaps Jacob practiced these principles in his outer life when he received the inner guidance always there in our meditations, dreams, meaningful visions, intuitions and picture language. Joseph Campbell says: *Our outward-oriented consciousness, addressed to the demands of the day, may lose touch with these inward forces.* This is true. Yet, if our allegiance to outward principles is sound and based in Truth, these Principles too will bring us home. True Principles are based on what God wants. Then the inner awareness springs in us to greater awareness of the Allness, the Almighty Presence.

Jacob, by an inner knowing, by an angelic being, by a messenger from God, received the word to change his name to Israel. Call his experience the result of inspired knowing, an act of Divine intervention; nevertheless, a heavenly angelic being or an internal mechanism we can't explain gave him this message: *Drop the name of Jacob and call yourself Israel.* The Bible defines Israel as "having power with God."

In the fullness of God's grace, cosmic events happen. The messenger and the message are One. The wave and the particle are celebrating and resonating at a higher frequency. Things happen that are difficult to explain. Only a fool would try to explain them. I am willing to look foolish for what I call a heavenly cause. The individuals who have given me permission to share some of their extraordinary experiences are secure enough within themselves. They are, indeed, gracious to share these precious events with us. I am sure that many events like these are kept private.

Our purpose is not flamboyant. Our desire is to be informative, provocative and occasionally humorous. I trust God is listening: Our mouths to Her ears.

Meditation

Meditation is something common to Archbishop Watters, Jacob and anyone else wanting to be proactive in their spiritual development. The story about Jacob's ladder is a story about how to raise one's spiritual awareness and bring it into earthly expression. Meditation Mount in Ojai, California, is a nondenominational teaching organization. They respect all religious convictions and offer free literature on the subject of meditation to anyone. There are many good books on the subject in libraries and bookstores. Trust your own judgment.

Meditation is a way to unblock the intuitive process; the rational mind is not enough by itself. It is to be used in concert with our intuitive faculty. The rational mind uses the discoveries of the intuitive mind. The rational mind and the intuitive mind are one mind, just as the particle and the wave contain the properties of the other. We can't have one without the other. In order to have white light we must have a particle and a wave. In order to let our light shine, we must use our rational and intuitive mind.

We could say the particle and the wave are like unto God. They exist everywhere and cannot be separated. The wave is like the movement of Spirit as Love and the particle is like the intelligence that gives to us experiential life, the Life of God in us as us. The particle is like a principle and the wave is like a presence. The inner-directed individual is choosing to explore Superconsciousness through meditation, dreams, intuition, the waves and vibrations of an inner knowing. The outer-directed individual is choosing to live a good life by using principles that are sound. Sound, in this respect, means they vibrate and resonate to infinite compassion and endless intelligence. Sound also means that the information comes through originally as inspired wisdom that we accept as vital and sacred today.

These principles from the book *Managing from the Heart* are vital aids but are not substitutes for cultivating an inner awareness. You may wish to practice these principles. They are good. Your belief system may get challenged by some idea expressed throughout this book or through the course of everyday living. Apply these principles and see how they work wonderfully in all situations. They are expressed as an acronym, displayed as follows:

HEAR AND UNDERSTAND ME.

EVEN IF YOU DISAGREE, PLEASE DON'T MAKE ME WRONG.

ACKNOWLEDGE THE GREATNESS WITHIN ME.

REMEMBER TO LOOK FOR MY LOVING INTENTIONS.

TELL ME THE TRUTH WITH COMPASSION.

How to Grow Spiritually

Involution is the key to expanded spiritual awareness. Whatever we do to make that *inner connection* to the Almighty helps us to evolve spiritually. Most religions have chants of invocation that help us get in touch with the Holy Spirit. Some Buddhists call this object of fundamental respect, and worthy of honor, *Gohonzan*. They practice chanting to enable them to manifest their inherent Buddha qualities. True Christians practice the presence of God in them as weil.

God of Israel, to whom David *sang* as a shepherd boy, and later as king, was in the Philistine giant as well. David slew the giant with a rock. An extraordinary event indeed—a shepherd boy had power over a giant! The Philistine giant represents the large egotistical chasm we create in our belief system that separates us from our

God-likeness. It was David's devotion and Love for Spirit that gave him the blessed assurance that God was guiding him. Of course, true courage is from the heart. The soul has awakened and acted to the will of the Divine Shepherd. One in God is a majority.

God is everywhere, present and nonexclusive. The extraordinary events that happen through us are meant to be. Extraordinary events for God must be easy and fit into the Divine Plan. In any event, there are numerous ways to invoke in our awareness the resemblance of God. Singing and chanting our love and devotion to God does enable the Good Shepherd to guide us in beneficial ways. It puts us in resonance with the object and subject of our chant. Chanting allows us to transcend our problems into elevated awareness. Like the story of Jacob's ladder, we can rise in consciousness, and come back to earth and transmute our everyday problems with extraordinary power from the Ever-Present One.

My niece Elaina suffered from major abuse as a child and carried it into her teens and young adult life through her own unenlightened momentum. Courts considered her an unfit mother and awarded her first child's custody to her husband. The husband used Elaina's vulnerability to obtain a child. He divorced her and returned to his barren first wife with a child they had always wanted.

Elaina, now in her early thirties, was a single parent until she recently married. Her second and third sons, Jacob and Matthew, are children from a relationship that lacked commitment. Elaina has given up her drug, alcohol, and people abuse. She has joined a sect of Buddhism that has taught her to chant meaningfully. Her sons sparkle and share the gifts of love that are most apparent in their mother. Elaina's new husband, John, introduced her to Buddhism and its spiritual practices while they were dating. John is the good male role-model that had escaped her till now. He introduced her to spiritual practices that enabled them to reach a sense of assurance that God is helping them.

Elaina was kind enough to provide many written testimonials that have changed lives dramatically through the practice of chanting. My good friend and first proofreader, Dorothy Boyer, chanted her way through a serious bout with cancer. She chanted the word HU, which is an ancient name for God. Her account and techniques are in my first book, *Licking Your Wounds*.

This extraordinary power that we discover and use is still a mystery to me. My confidence grows in the intuition application of this power as reliable feedback validates my use of it. Such is illustrated in the next example.

Healing Is a Mystery

Some ten years ago, I was in business negotiations with two friends, Jack and Marilyn. We formed a partnership to buy some property. Marilyn developed a headache, and I asked her if she would like me to do a healing treatment with her. We went into a room for privacy. She sat on a chair. I had her relax and asked her permission to pray as I placed my hands over her head.

A mysterious, intuitive flash passed through my mind. I call it mysterious because I was a novice at paying attention to intuitive impressions and feelings. I have since learned they are the soft messages from Deity, and that God is everywhere present and absolutely for us. As I felt this message, I knew I needed to verbalize it for Marilyn.

The message was, "Marilyn, you have suffered much from your addictions to alcohol and Valium. God is going to show you how to use your suffering to help others. This is your key to wholeness. Your cure will enable you to serve God in this way."

Approximately six months later, I visited Marilyn at a hospital. Marilyn had confined herself there. She wanted to overcome her addiction to a legalized drug. She told me her withdrawals from this drug made hell seem like a reality. Her pain and suffering and hallucinations were more intense from Valium than previously from alcohol.

I lost contact with Marilyn for about eight years. Today I received an autographed copy of a book which Marilyn co-authored with Drusilla Campbell. The book, published in 1988, had sold very well. It is an easy-to-read textbook for managers called *Drugs and Alcohol in the Workplace*. Yes, God as Spirit knew that Marilyn Graham had within her a strong desire to serve. First, she got herself well. Secondly, she listened and felt for guidance. Thirdly, she acted upon her intuitive knowing.

Within a few years of the healing treatment, Marilyn was helping, teaching, coaching and writing without benefit or hindrance of a college degree. God is so Good and can do anything through us as we become aware of each holy instant in our lives!

God is life. All healing comes through God. Wellness is the whole, true image and likeness of us as conceived in the eternal Truth of our being. Disease and suffering are experiential and are distortions of our true being. Disease and suffering are clarion calls to wholeness. Through the grace of God we, like Marilyn, usually awaken gradually. What does God want from us? We are to love and serve one another as a beneficial presence to the world and all of its inhabitants. Let us learn to live on the frontier of forever.

PART II

GET A LIFE: ON THE FRONTIER OF FOREVER

EACH OF US has an internal guidance system that can
access any portion of the cosmic whole. The cosmic
universe has unbounded frontiers and limitless possibilities. Our spirit has direct access to Universal Spirit. Love
is the software program that opens the portals to the
Frontier of Forever. Law is a guidance system which en-
hances our spiritual awareness. As students of Truth, we
seek to align ourselves with what we understand God is.

What does it mean to live on the Frontier of Forever?
It means as we come to know, love and serve God, we
realize our essential nature is an expression of the Divine.
It means that God is eternally expressing Self through all
creation, including us. God as Spirit provides all the
resources that we require to discover more of Itself on
the Frontier of Forever. The extraordinary experiences
shared in this book brought each of us to new frontiers
of self.

In a sense, all of us are pioneers on the Frontier of
Forever.

Direct Experience of God

Mystics, saints and sages do not wait for a life hereafter to have a direct experience of God. In the vernacular, "Get a life" is a way of telling someone to *get real*. The desire body within our heart is ruled by the way we think. If we think we are here to please someone else, or to make someone else's life miserable, we are playing a flat note, off key. To *get real* is to realize we are here for God. If we want to play a whole note on key, it takes practice. We must have an idea, a concept, a sense of what is whole, perfect and complete within us. What is God? How do we bond with the Almighty?

Saint Teresa of Avila tells us this: *The moment of what is called a spiritual ecstasy is a part of the experience of the bonding of the heart whereby the soul can no longer be separated from her Lord.* The Lord or Law of our being is ruled by our heart. If we are going to honor the melody resident within our own heart, the lyrics would read *To thine own Self be true; there is no other.*

English Lady Is True to Her Calling

I opened my heart to write a book about extraordinary events happening to ordinary people. While visiting a bookstore in Hong Kong, I told the proprietor of my intention to accumulate spiritual-awareness experiences of others. She offered to put my request in the store's newsletter. Much to my surprise, the first response came from a lady in England, Mrs. Stella Horrocks.

Stella is a most interesting lady who had a near-death experience while in the hospital. This is an extraordinary experience for the one having it. It is a very commonly reported experience today. When one has a glimpse of the Frontier of Forever, it often results in a pivotal life change. For over 20 years, Stella has been an automatic writer. Automatic writing in her case means that her hand will be writing one subject while she is carrying on a conversation or reading aloud on an entirely different subject. She says, ''Spirits write through my hand.'' There are obviously two minds at work simultaneously using the same body. This is proving to Stella and any observers that there are two different minds at work. Her spirit cooperates with a spirit who has passed on to another dimension of life but has some unfinished business in this life.

An Australian company interviewed her for a television program called *Extraordinary Folks*. Stella has written six novels plus many short stories. To Stella, acting as a medium or channel for well-known authors who have passed on is not an extraordinary thing. After all, she has been doing it for twenty of her 68 years in this body.

Stella warns us in later correspondence that it is not a good idea to pursue the spirit world since there are un-enlightened spirits as well as wise ones. An old song lyric says, ''Don't mess with mister in-between.'' The world of good and kind spirits does work through some of us.

This arrangement is made in a place she calls *Eternity*, long before we enter this expression of life. "If a person is chosen to work for both worlds [human and spirit], he or she is trained in Eternity. That is, they are trained to receive the work, trained to have patience, and above all, trained to trust in the highly evolved spirit." Now Stella shares one of her chance encounters.

Chance Encounter

In one of Stella's automatic writing sessions, the name Brenda M. came up: "Find Brenda M." Brenda M. was an old school friend of fifty years before. Stella had run into her old friend once twenty years later, for five minutes.

Stella got on board a bus the day after this automatic writing session. Soon she realized she was on the wrong bus. She asked the stranger sitting next to her, "Pardon me, could you tell me the number of this bus?" The stranger replied, "Please don't think it impertinent, but you have the voice of an old friend of mine, a Stella Horrocks. My name is Brenda Middleton." Stella found out that Brenda almost never took the bus and usually traveled by car.

What is it that brings us together in chance encounters? What is it that brings a long-lost friend to mind and mysteriously the next day we encounter them? There is a dynamic guidance within Life. A power for Good, in the Universal Mind of God, is always for us. There are no chance encounters or accidents. Destiny is the evolutionary future of all previous choices. The more attuned we are to what Spirit is urging us to do and then do it, the more fulfilled we are.

Principle and Presence Reemphasized

Forever in accordance with Divine Will, each of us must decide and choose the music that is correct for us in the Divine Melody of Life. The tune playing itself through me is that God is Love, God is Principle and Presence. We practice the principles and live in the Presence. This is what brings us to the Frontier of Forever expressing in accordance with divine Love and Law. The Principle is like the words we put to a song, and the Presence is like the melody resident within the tune.

The principles we choose to live by may look like the Ten Commandments, the Eightfold Path of the Buddha, the Way of the Tao, or Christ's principle of Love. The purpose of practicing these is to teach us to become more aware of the Divine Presence. As my friend Danita says, *We walk the talk.* Homer Johnson used to say, *I take it to the Man upstairs.* Homer was an extraordinary person. He made a good living praying very effectively for others. He used a proven, scientific method of praying called *Spiritual Mind Treatment.*

Foundation for Understanding
Spiritual Mind Treatment

Spiritual Mind Treatment is a proven five-step process that enables us to express our full potential well-being in areas of our life that seem to be lacking in it.

Whatever seems to lack in our own expression of life comes out of an immature understanding of what our full potential truly is. Only God knows what our full potential really is. Only Spirit has a whole, perfect and complete image of each of us.

The good news is that we can access the mind of God and thus discover God's understanding of our full potential. The difficult news to accept is, *we can have only what we can accept.* Acceptance of our full potential depends upon our readiness to attune ourselves with the mind of God. There is an order of growth to our progress in the understanding of what God is and is not. V. Vernon Woolf, Ph.D., has developed a fantastic mind-model that shows the order of growth to our full potential well be-ing. Dr. Woolf says, "*Our Full-Potential-Self exists NOW.* It is the 'I' within us which acts as a built-in blueprint, guides our growth, and orchestrates all kinds of events in our lives." I have referenced his book *Holodynamics*, which contains the six stages of growth in a mind-model, in the Bibliography.

This notion of progressive stages of God Consciousness is described in the biblical metaphor which states, "In my father's house there are many mansions." Mansions represent stages of development. There is a natural order of development or growth. And there is a way to realize and accelerate the growth process. The realization within our consciousness of our Full-Potential-Self is likened to the sun, water, soil and air that harmonically provide for the seed all that it needs to mature. Here are other biblical clues: ''Apply thine heart to understanding'' (Proverbs 2:2), and ''When wisdom entereth into thy heart, and knowledge is pleasant unto thy soul'' (Proverbs 2:10). Dr. Woolf uses a technique called *Tracking*. Tracking exemplifies the practical application of the bibilical passages. Tracking is similar to, but different from, Spiritual Mind Treatment. Both techniques require us to access our Full-Potential-Self. The full-potential solution is always present within the problem. You will get a sense of the results of Tracking in the next story, ''Transformation of Terrorists'' (see p. 62).

If we are to understand the application of Tracking or Spiritual Mind Treatment, it is useful to have an awareness of God as Principle and God as Presence. We can know God as Principle because as mature wisdom enters into our consciousness, something in us understands the intrinsic ''Good'' in the expressed Principle, such as the Principle of Love. We can't touch Love but we can understand It. On the other hand we *can* be touched by Love. We can sense Love's Presence. We can intuitively feel the ''Good.'' We, the observer, can know the Principle and sense the Presence. This is the knowledge (Principle) that is pleasant to the soul (mind) and the wisdom that entereth the heart (Presence) found in the biblical book Proverbs. This is not such a mystical journey after all. It is a practical appreciation for divine unfoldment of our Full-Potential Self. There is a trilogy in the foundation of all Life. We can observe it as Principle/Presence/Effect. Effect is the observable condition, the form.

In quantum physics, we understand this trilogy theory as Particle/Wave/Observer. Interaction of the particle and the wave is influenced by the consciousness of the observer. The *particle* represents that which is the linear, calculative, judgmental, processed in the left hemisphere of the cerebral cortex. The *wave* represents the unlimited creativity of all possibilities, reflecting the right cerebral cortex function. Consciousness (the observer) is the dynamic awareness of something as it is, or as it really is. The observer has freedom of choice to accept limitation, or to access the full-potential blueprint in the Holodynamics of what really is the full potential waiting to be manifested. Holodynamics is the dynamic expression of the whole of Life, from the micro to the macro, like a multidimensional, multilevel hologram. The Holodynamic contains the past, present and future in the now.

Intuitive knowing is important to realizing our full potential expression of well-being. Affirming, making firm the experience of well-being in consciousness, acts as a generator of experiencing *at-one-ment*. The Principle/Presence/Effect and the Particle/Wave/Observer are in alignment with the resemblance of our mature holodyne. The mature holodyne is the multidimensional informational system that contains the entire "blueprint" of well-being. The Spiritual Mind practitioner accesses the resemblance of well-being in treatment and affirms it as Truth.

All physical, personal, interpersonal and social well-being resides in the whole, perfect and complete mind of God and can be intuitively realized. This is what Jesus called the "kingdom." The kingdom comes into our consciousness through our intuitive faculty. Our intuitive faculty knows our full-potential well-being from an infinite perspective. Our intuition accesses the direct revelation of Truth in concert with mature holodynes.

Students of Truth

As students of Truth we are aware of the value in developing our intuitive faculties. It gives us the understanding to make the spiritually mature choices that produce an effective Spiritual Mind Treatment. The more spiritual or God-like the mentality of the practitioner, the more powerful the treatment.

Ernest Holmes, the founder of Science of Mind philosophy and teacher extraordinaire of Spiritual Mind Treatment, stated that "the one who attempts to heal himself or another through a recognition of the creative power of Mind and the ever availability of Good, is a mental or spiritual practitioner."

Our Mind-Processing Dynamic

Our particle, or linear, mind works in concert with the wave or the unlimited imagination. Our conscious mind chooses to express its full potential and then checks with the intuitive mind, which in turn consults with our *Full-Potential-Self*.

Spiritual Mind Treatment

Spiritual Mind Treatment is a five-step process that aids us in reaching our full potential spiritually, mentally, emotionally and physically. These steps can be used by anyone and they have helped ordinary people achieve extraordinary results. Perhaps it is the next step for you. Here is the procedure.

Find a quiet location where you can be without interruption for fifteen minutes. You have a choice: either lie down, or sit down with your back erect. Get comfortable. Close your eyes. Go to your imaginative place of peace (a beach, mountains or any natural place of beauty or comfort to you). If you have any guides, mentors or friends in this world or the next, you may ask for their support of unconditional love and acceptance of the five steps you are about to undertake. When you feel you are ready, begin the five steps of Spiritual Mind Treatment. These are recognition, unification, realization, thanksgiving and release.

The Five Steps of Spiritual Mind Treatment

Recognition: God as One Mind, One Presence, One Life, One Spirit, and One Power.

Unification: I am an individualization of God, as a beam of light is to the sun, as a drop of water is to the ocean, as a part is to the whole. I move and have my being in the unlimited totality of Infinite Love and Boundless Intelligence.

Realization: I realize through the grace of God the full potential of me and I understand the transformational process. I gladly accept my part in the Universal Plan. I courageously take the next step and know my part is pertinent to the Good of the whole.

Thanksgiving: I give thanks to thee, Almighty God, Everlasting and True.

Release: I release my dynamic thought forms into the Universal Mind of God, knowing that they are fully empowered to demonstrate the desired results, rendering their full potential; I let go and let the Universal Good prevail.

These five steps in treatment become more effective as *you choose your words,* which generate the feeling of Universal Oneness, and Attunement to Unconditional Love. The Spiritual Mind Treatment is a process by which deep "blueprints" of our Full-Potential-Being are converted into surface structure. The holodyne's mature image of a Full-Potential-Self is contained in the genetic material from one cell to another waiting to be realized.

The realization of this Truth by the Spiritual Mind practitioner is already known by the Full-Potential-Self of the recipient. Bingo!—the healing is complete. Thank you, God.

The metaphor of the apple seed shows us that the whole is in the seed. The seed has within it a whole, perfect and complete apple tree. We students of Truth are learning all that is required of us to honor the seed of full potential within ourselves and others. As we learn to do this, we realize we can harvest the extraordinary fruits of full-potential well-being now. Dr. Woolf is an extraordinary facilitator of cultivating the field for the seed of full potential to mature, even in the most difficult situations. Some of Dr. V. Vernon Woolf's examples follow, under the heading "Transformation of Terrorists."

Transformation of Terrorists

A few days ago, I walked the streets of Nablus in the Golan Heights area of what used to be Syria and is now part of the occupied territory of Israel. Nablus is the stronghold of the Palestine resistance to occupation. These native people are under siege. I witnessed soldiers shooting indiscriminately down into the streets of men and women and children in Nablus. I barely escaped the bullets which put holes in the awning just above my head, not ten feet away. Over 110,000 young people have been wounded or killed by the soldiers in the past 36 months. It is worse than a Holocaust, it's genocide. It is justified because of the hate within the hearts of the so-called terrorists—well, I met with the terrorists.

One was Muhammad. Both of his arms were broken irreparably and all of his fingers could bend back to the wrists. He had been imprisoned when he was five, born and raised under occupation without laws of any kind, without the right to do business, own property or even be protected by the Geneva Convention rules. This young man has continued to resist the death sentence declared by the ruling regime. He has been in prison time after time and has been tortured beyond endurance, all because he wants to live in peace and have a home of his own. While Muhammad was filled with hate, he had the heart of a terrorist. As we explored his hate (holodyne), he described it as a great black cloud that filled his universe. He was looking for solutions, so he agreed to be "tracked." (*Tracking* means to go into the holodyne that is expressing hate and receive its positive intent message.) As we entered this cloud we were able to explore its intent. It wanted to destroy the world.

Muhammad was very sad; he saw no way out. As we tracked the cloud, beneath it was the desire for peace. The process took time, but we got to his *Full-Potential-Self*. What we found was a light so great that he called it the power of heaven within him. Muhammad became in front of my eyes a different being. He understood the reason for his suffering. It was to make him strong. He understood why he was born under such inhuman and oppressive occupation. It was so he could be an ambassador for peace. He loved peace more than anyone else I know. When he finished, he was wringing wet. The transformation was real for him.

He found his inner source. His Full-Potential-Self now guides him in his daily activities. He has switched from resistance and hate to cooperating and love. He's a great example for all of us. We were able to facilitate this type of transformation in terrorist after terrorist. Then we met with the Israelis. We slept in the kibbutzes, shared their dreams and visions for their country. They too are filled with hate. They too want peace. We met together with Arab and Israeli. One group had been meeting together for three years, which was very taboo in their society. It's not condoned. But they had never agreed on anything. They met, they said, just to meet. They had agreed to disagree.

During the meeting I asked one of the Arabs to stand. Then I asked each Arab and each Israeli in the group—there were about thirty people present—to imagine this Arab's Full-Potential-Self. It took only a moment, and everyone was participating. The Arab soon felt very good. Then I asked one of the Cabinet members from the nation of Israel who is also a member of the group, to stand. We did the same for him. He, too, felt very good after a few moments. Then I asked them to face each other, eye to eye—the Arab and the Israeli—and imagine each other at their Full-Potential. They started to cry and hug each other and kiss each other on the cheeks.

In this frame of mind, Full-Potential-Self to Full-Potential-Self, we can solve all problems. When people relate, Full-Potential to Full-Potential, it is possible to maximize potential. Not only does it work in overcoming our so-called unsolvable problems, like terrorism, war, drug abuse, depression, and, emotional stress, but it is even effective for rehabilitation of known criminals. These processes work inside of prisons and hospitals but they even work better in prevention. And that's where you come in. It also works when dealing with your friends and family and social groups and business associates.

This story came from the cassette tape by V. Vernon Woolf, Ph.D., which accompanies his booket *The Full-Potential-Self Mindbook*, published in 1991.

This processing that Dr. Woolf refers to is called *Track-ing*. Like Spiritual Mind Treatment, it can be learned. One place to begin to understand the foundation of Tracking is in Dr. Woolf's book *Holodynamics*. It is published by Harbinger House (Tucson, Ariz.). Dr. Woolf expects to train 2000 trainers by the year 2000. Maybe this is the next step for you?

It is my joy to have experienced Holodynamic Training and the Tracking method on myself and others. The results are extraordinary and beneficial to the participants. My next step will be to further develop my training skill in Holodynamics.

Divine Presence

We must get out of our little sense of self and feel that we are in an individual expression of Divine Presence. Not from an inflated sense of self-worth but from a realization that God is all there is. To know God we must live in attunement with our essential nature.

The story of Jacob in the Bible is the story of moving from self-consciousness to Godlike-awareness. Jacob climbed the ladder in a dreamlike, meditative rise to the Frontier of Forever. The melody played there is a resemblance of Divine Presence. The Divine Presence brings into the world the harmonics of Love, Joy, Peace and Abundance. Realization of these attributes of God can be discerned by students of Truth. To live it is to become aware that we are it. As a ray is to the sun, as a note is to a song, so our part is vital to the whole.

Godlike Awareness

Jacob raised his consciousness to Godlike awareness. Yes, he had to struggle with the disorientated tone of his lower self to become aware of Divine Presence. Through prayer, meditation and living in accord with the highest principles, Jacob attained an enlightened awareness. He felt the omnipresence of God expressing through him as him. He was given the name *Israel*. Why? Because he did something extraordinary well, Jacob was enabled to transform his lower nature, using the resident nature of the Divine Presence. Jacob could not do it alone. He learned to cooperate and to keep the covenant with God.

Hear, O Israel: there is but One life, One mind, One power, and One presence. This Presence is expressing itself everywhere in its triad nature as Spirit-Mind-Body. Truly I say unto us, God is Love expressing through Law. The principles we practice are intrinsically known. They bring our awareness into at-one-ment, and our essential divinity is known. We are using a divine law to bring us into the resemblance of Divine Presence. Thus, the Phoenix rises out of the ashes of the ordinary into the extraordinary. At the new frontier of our mind, the Eternal is revealing some more of Itself through us, as us, and so on, and so on, and so on. It is forever expanding our exploration into inner and outer space as self discovers Self.

Law of Attraction

I just received the following information in the mail: *Every day and every hour we are meeting the eternal realities of life, and in such degree as we cooperate with these eternal realities in love, in peace, in wisdom, and in joy—believing and receiving—we are automatically blessed. Our prayer is answered before it is uttered,* per Ernest Holmes as quoted in a Science of Mind Foundation letter published May 31, 1994. Thank you, God. The information is assimilated and harmonically converged, because what we give our interest to is drawn to us, as we are to it. That is the key to affirmative thinking. Yes, like Jacob we are to cultivate the enlightened way of attuning our lesser thoughts to the ones that affirm Truth. We need to sort out the "junk mail" of our mind and access or act upon that which we know is God-centered. The will-to-good is God-centered. As we succeed in aligning ourselves with the Truth of being in the world for God, like Jacob, we are given the name *Israel.*

Israel means "enlightened" and "having power with God." It is also a symbolic name that recognizes the three aspects of divinity in one God. *Is is derived from the Egyptian word Isis. Ra* is the Egyptian word for sun god. *El* is the ancient Hebrew word for God the Father. Symbolizing the divine Mother, Isis gave virgin birth to a divine Son through the will of an infinite Father. Is Ra El is a key to how one gains God's power through the law of attunement.

There is a blessing intended to bring to our attention how Spirit works through its triune nature. The blessing is *In the name of the Father, and of the Son, and of the Holy Spirit Mother.* The priest/priestess raises his or her hand and makes the sign of the cross as he or she says these or similar words. The vertical movement meets at the horizontal axis. At the center or axis is the attunement of the transpersonal with the personal. It is where the Son of God meets the son of man* symbolically on the cross. It is a place in consciousness where the self is true to the Self.

Law of Attunement

God the Father is our use of Superconscious mind. God the Mother is impregnated with the living Word. The God seed or thought is unadulterated. It enters the fertile womb of our unconscious mind (creative medium). God's thoughts, God's words are immaculate. Our minds are immaculately conceived, and as the divine thought or word materializes, it is called *Immanuel*, the Divine Son. For example, the word *Love* is a symbol for God. It is a Principle and a Presence. Jesus taught us this. He called the Principle *the Father within* and the Presence *the Holy Comforter.* The Holy Comforter is the Divine Feminine which nurtures the spiritual Truth, like Love, into expression. The Son, called *Israel*, is the one who cor-

---

*Here, as elsewhere, the words *son*, *man*, are not intended to denote the masculine gender but are employed solely for reasons of historical usage or else to avoid elaborate and awkward frames of reference.

rectly interprets the Divine impulse, and regularly expresses It. That individual is being here for God and has discovered God's power through alignment with Spirit.

Sacred Sites

The creative process is constantly working through us to expand our awareness of *how* it works through us.

A few weeks ago I took a colleague from Chicago with me to the Temple La Luce at Mexicali in Mexico. Danita, a fortyish African American, is a minister who walks the talk of Love. She practices the principles and, fortunately, speaks Spanish.

It was 8:45 A.M. when we arrived unannounced at the Temple of Light (English translation). I introduced Danita to Rev. Margarita Felix who runs the place. I immediately prepared myself to serve Holy Communion at the 9:00 service and asked Danita to help me.

I usually make this journey to Mexicali a few times per year. I have a great deal of respect for the healing work that takes place there. A strong vibration of Peace permeates the air. It is a testimony to the people who pray, sing and meditate on an infinite Presence. Any sacred site is conducive to healing because the vibrations of Love there are coupled with the belief in greater ''Good.'' Remember the Law of Attraction: as we put faith in something greater than we are, we attract it to ourselves. This is not to say God is outside of us. Spirit works through us in very definite ways.

True, unobstructed, unobscured insight is the sacred

place or site of the Almighty within us. How we think determines the outcome of what we express. The ordinary converges into the extraordinary. Godlike realization arises.

How Dense Can I Be?

About an hour into the Catholic service, where we said the rosary and sang spiritual songs, we celebrated Communion. As I was distributing the communion, I noticed a young Mexican lady with tears in her eyes staring at me. Later, at the end of the servcice, people are often invited to share their spiritual experiences. This same young lady (I'll call her Maria) had something important to tell us. I needed to have Maria's story translated and repeated to me three times. Her shared experience was so profound it hammered away at my limited belief system. My mind was being exposed to a spiritual frontier rarely visited by this pioneer.

Maria Spoke Truth

Maria shared a direct experience of how Spirit works through her. It went like this:

> My mother was paralyzed all down the right side of her body. I prayed for her healing and fell asleep alongside my invalid mother. I had a dream. In my dream I came to a house, knocked on the door, and it opened. I saw a

man standing in a room filled with vertical light rays. He was the same man who served communion to us today in the Temple of Light, Padre Sommer. When I awoke from my dream, my mother was much better. My mother is seated over there, near Padre Sommer. She is healed.

Here is the part that stretched my belief system. Maria went on to say:

I have never been to the Temple of Light before today, and I had never been acquainted with Padre Sommer in any way.

Although Rev. Margarita explained it to me three times and my friend Danita verified the accuracy of the translation, it took me time to bridge this new frontier. My mind is expanding to accept truth as it is. In some mysterious way, Spirit uses us to do the work. It is also true that I give God permission to use me as an instrument of healing and as a minister of Love and Light. It is the evolution of the soul back into the awareness of the Oversoul, the ordinary into the extraordinary. Jesus said, *My Father worketh hitherto, and I work* (John 5:17)—working in the context of unity, knowing the Self to be an individualization of the whole.

Intellect and Feeling Nature

Left-brain people may use more of their intellect and logic to discover God as Principle. A masculine Power knows the truth of being as an immaculate concept, the image and likeness of Itself. Intellectual beings can understand love as a principle and as the will of God, as in *Thy will be done*—the resonant melody intellectually expressed in the lyrics, "Love Me, and Love One Another."

Willingly God gives us the freedom of choice but not freedom from the consequences of our choices. God is conscious Intelligence expressing boundless Love. God is that which is beyond description and transcends duality. God knows the Self as One. There is no other.

We can learn to vibrate holistically to the Divine cadence. Our thinking can be harmonic or discordant. We do have the power of will to choose, to use our intellect in beneficial ways.

We use the right side of our brain to approach Spirit. We are cultivating and using our feeling nature. It is the feminine nature to be intuitive, to be caring, nurturing, and empathic. It is the sincere act of forgiveness. The Divine Feminine is always *giving of Itself*. It is our complete surrender of a separate self, a sublime remembrance, a total indulgence in being here as an individualization of God. It is the creative medium that turns thoughts, emotions and feelings into things. It is the blind Intelligence of the law of Cause and Effect. It is God as Presence, the impartial and impersonal application of karmic law, the Universal Subjective Mind acting in concert with the Divine Masculine. This is absolute Wisdom expressing Itself.

Importance of Balance

Balance is important. What we willingly give our attention to shows up in our experience. The Divine Feminine has no choice but to give birth to what we think about with feeling. That is why we need to replace our negative thoughts with God-centered thoughts.

Marsha Sinetar in her book *Ordinary People As Monks and Mystics* (p. 175) says:

> The inner journey, whatever its cost, and whatever form it takes, is necessary for anybody who wishes to embody in thought, word and action all that he truly loves. In this way, he comes to know and to be his ideally balanced, most wholesome and generous self: his highest Self.

Pivotal Key

When we are out of balance, we are not in resonance with the Absolute. God does not play off key, create discord or disease. We do. *We* are discordant. *We* are off key. We get back on key by forgiving ourselves and others of our ignorance. But we are ignoring what God wants.

A leap of faith, greater understanding and deliberate attentiveness to both the divine Masculine and Divine Feminine within ourselves is a pivotal key. The key unlocks the portal to the resident Spirit. God shows us the way to balance harmonic ways of living in the world. We can condition the mind to know the Mind, and the heart will be open and the way made straight.

Suffering Artist

A distant relative I met some fifty years ago in Canada arrived at my Southern California home. I'll call her Rose. Rose is now sixty-five years old and she is an artist. It is hard to believe she just obtained her first driver's license. She drove out here from the East Coast, some three thousand miles. This was her first driving experience. When she parked five feet from my curb, I wondered how she had survived the long drive.

Rose showed me some of her artwork; she had an obvious talent. I would like to examine more of her work to see if it reflects the anger she had toward her parents, particularly her father. Rose says she was abused as a child, rejected by her father. She said her father was abusive to her mother as well. The mother did not have the courage to leave him. There was no financial or emotional support for her to do so. Rose was a rebellious child who did not fit the prim, proper and prosperous ideal of her Canadian parents.

Rose said she was dumped on the streets of New York City at age eleven and was forced to live with relatives in New Jersey for a few years. She then made her home in New York's Greenwich Village. She later lived with a black man and had a son. At that point, even her brothers and sister disowned her.

Rose later lived with a white man of Italian descent whom she eventually married, and had a daughter. She grew up with her daughter, and they became the best of friends. Rose drove to California to attend her daughter's graduation. Her daughter had encouraged her to attend art school many years ago. Although her art-school teacher and others encouraged her over the years to display her work in a gallery, she would not. Rose is so embittered toward her father and disappointed with her mother that she made it her rule never to please them. "I will never give my parents the satisfaction of my success. I will not be successful while they live" was her core cry. (By the way, the settlement from the death of Rose's parents' estate provided her with the funds, at age sixty-five, to buy her first car *and provided the funds that enabled her to hold her first public showing of many years of accumulated artwork.*) No doubt her power-filled thoughts of resentment contributed to her developing cancer. Her "no success" consciousness was a self-fulfilling prophecy.

Yet, a part of Rose worked to help people less fortunate. Greenpeace was one cause she supported in the Los Angeles area. She also helped the indigent, the hungry and the homeless. The Divine Spark urges us to give lovingly and creatively of ourselves.

Divine Spark

We all have a Divine Spark fueled by the almighty Life Force within Itself. It is a resident guidance system that brings us to remembrance of Itself.

Rose, the struggling and suffering artist, had an extraordinary experience. Here is what happened:

I noticed at the Port of Call at the Los Angeles dock the listless body of a young man. Upon closer inspection the bearded youth was undernourished, dissipated, very thin and probably homeless. I roused him into a conversation, and much to my surprise the young man was my nephew.

Yes, Rose greeted the young man and asked his name. He responded with her brother's name. He was the namesake and eldest son of her prosperous brother Ed. Rose was astounded, almost dumbfounded. Finding her nephew in this poor condition after all these years was shocking—a nephew she hardly knew because her brother refused to have anything to do with her. What was the Divine Spark doing? Is this a Cosmic joke? What brought an unwanted aunt together with a homeless, helpless nephew?

It was the Divine Artist orchestrating a serendipitous meeting between a down-and-out nephew and a black-sheep aunt. What could they possibly learn from one another?

History Repeats Itself

History repeats itself with endless certainty. Rose's nephew, Ed, was estranged from his dad. Ed became a mirror image of Rose's hateful relationship with her deceased father. He was also an image of her self-imposed poverty consciousness. Her nephew and his financially prosperous father deliberately had no contact with each other. They lived three thousand miles apart. Yet it was animosity that really kept them distant from each other.

Rose can now allow herself to become successful, since her parents have died. The Divine Spark may seem to be suppressed, but life will repeat with an endless fury the lesson we need to learn. True Love is everywhere present and will use extraordinary measures to bring us into remembrance of Itself. *What God wants for us can only happen through us.*

A very talented young Russian violinist, Anne-Sophie Mutter, said in an interview on TV, *An artist [a violinist] is like an artificial flower if you only know music. One must be a well-rounded person to be a genuine flower.* Intellectual discipline without heart restricts the Divine Impulse to Love. It is Principle without Presence—a demigod expression of wholeness, like a religious person who keeps the rules but has no compassion. God wants us to remember our wholeness. True success is living wholeheartedly.

The Lady from Cambria

The power of compassion is most evident in the grandmother, the lady from Cambria, "Mo" Hainer. Mo is a strange name, yet a very welcomed name in the field of death and dying. She is a tireless worker in the AIDS community.

Mo and her husband were driving down the highway and came upon on an accident. While her husband stopped the traffic, she went over to the accident victims. The mother, sprawled out on the road, had died. Her young son had a head injury. A mass of his forehead skin lay near him on the road. She comforted the unconscious boy and held his head in her hands and began to pray. She felt a stream of energy move through her hands. Some would call it White Light.

The next day, Mo called the hospital. The nurse said the boy was fine and his dad took him home.

Always in Our Right Place

Mo's story reminded me of the time my son Charles got lost. Charles took the wrong highway and stumbled upon a large tractor trailer that had just turned over in a remote area of central California. His CPR training as a Lifeguard gave him the tools to save the truckdriver's life. When the ambulance finally arrived, the attendants acknowledged that Charles probably saved his life. For the truckdriver, Charles was not lost; he was in his right place.

Young Vatican Deacon Wrestles with Celibacy

Deacon Juan Moreno, a young man once stationed at the Vatican in Rome, writes:

> My heart longed for the secure life behind the Rule of St. Ignatius, but my high sexual appetite drove me to dis-

YOUNG VATICAN DEACON WRESTLES WITH CELIBACY   79

traction. Celibacy was a high price to pay, or maybe not;
maybe this was the sacrifice to make.

Deacon Juan spent six months in prayer and discussed
his dilemma with a close friend. He studied the tempta-
tions of Jesus in the desert. Juan spent an hour a day in
meditation asking for guidance. He writes:

> I tried church after church, but in the midst of prayer,
> Spirit kept leading me into a quieter place by saying,
> "Follow me into the desert. There I will lead you by still
> water."

Three months later in January, in his cold, damp room
at 11:11 P.M., the sound of a slammed door jolted him
as he was dozing off in front of his philosophy book. He
decided to go down to the main chapel. In his haste he
went two levels below the basement. Deacon Juan was
now in a small subterranean chapel. In the dim flicker-
ing light coming from an old Byzantine oil lamp, he saw
no chairs or adornments. Juan pulled up an old musty-
smelling cushion and sat in the silence. He began his
prayer by saying, "Into your hands, Lord, I commend
my Spirit."
Deacon Juan writes:

> The next thing I remember was dreaming of a row of
> palm trees in the middle of the desert; a canal full of blue-
> green water next to a field of luscious, green grass; and
> two hands opening a curtain to let me see the wonders
> before me. A voice softly said, "Follow me into the

desert . . . and I will give water." When I awoke I felt
so refreshed.

I put in a request to be sent to the desert to the
province that I came from, Calexico, California. In six
months' time I was transferred to Calexico. Within
another six months, I decided happily to leave the order.
Three months later I met the woman I was to marry.

One day I stood on a hill looking out over Imperial
Valley where Calexico is located and a thought came to
me. All that I was given in my dream in Rome was here
in Calexico. The lush green fields, the canals, the rows
of palm trees. I had come home to the desert, and I thirst
no more.

The sexual urge in our libido is the seat of our creative center. This center creates more than sperm and egg.
Too often we think education is only the digesting of information to the detriment of the growth of our creative
impulses. The student of Truth must honor the creative
drive as well as take in information.

Present Generation

The present generation needs to know the solutions are
always found in the problems. It takes our Full-Potential-
Self to delve courageously into the challenges life offers.
It takes courage, skill and determination to grow in the
Spirit. We all have a purpose for being here. Do we know
what it is?

Is it not the heart that longs for its creative fulfillment?

The mind looks to find security in the world. It is the heart that finds its source in Spirit. We commonly say that a person has a lot of heart, or a great deal of courage. The root of the word *courage* is the word *heart*. The Bible says to worship God in Spirit. Love is Spirit. To know God and reveal Self as Love is easier to say than to do.

The deacon in us would like to live behind the rules of the establishment, never risking the creative fulfillment that our heart so longs to express. The Spirit recognized a priest, a teacher, a scholar in Deacon Juan, as well as the husband and father he has now become. Deacon Juan's struggle is not unlike our struggle to know and serve God. Do we take frequent, planned quiet time to attune ourselves to Spirit?

That which we search for in the desert is the pure, unadulterated joy in the seed of creative fulfillment. It often takes much quiet prayer and meditation to tune into what God wants. Water represents Spirit as that nourishing quality of Life Force—a Life Force which brings forth the bountiful seeds of creation within in the desert of our still, quiet mind.

As we learn to relax in the Spirit, joy often bubbles to the surface and in a moment we lighten up.

Laughter Is a Godlike Remedy for Seriousness

We all know laughter is good medicine, and science says it creates endorphins that sustain good health. Endorphins are Mother Nature's way of greatly reducing the sensation of pain in the brain. Laughter is a Godlike remedy for seriousness.

My son and I were visiting my gravely ill mother. Sometimes it gets difficult to accept the fact that we are here but a short time, or that a dear friend is suffering. My mother had cancer, an illness long familiar to me.

My thirty-one-year-old son Rob and I were sitting on my mother's couch. My niece Elaina's five-year-old son, Jake, wanted to know which of us was the older. Jake knew that my son was 31. I decided not to tell Jake that I was 58. Instead, I asked Jake to guess first. Jake said I was 135! My son Rob almost fell off the couch with laughter. When Rob stopped laughing, Jake with the straight face and timing of Bob Hope asked Rob, "Is 31 older than 135?" It was my turn to laugh hysterically.

What is it that prompts a child to ask questions so innocently with the skill of a seasoned comedian? For most of us, to be of good cheer requires deliberate effort in the face of adversity. *The Golden Key is not to take ourselves or adversity too seriously, to get out of our heads and into our hearts.* Tune into the infinite heart of Spirit which knows only Itself as Love, Joy and Peace.

Seven-Year-Old Girl Predicts Her Death

I met an attractive lady in the car-wash today. She told me her seven-year-old daughter predicted her own death. She was an extraordinarily aware child. She came home from school one day and asked her mother, "Do you know what the sharpest thing in the world is? It is a person's tongue." At seven she told her mother how difficult it was for her not to swear because all the kids were doing it. This child recognized the importance of positive and negative thoughts.

This perfectly well child told her mother something bad was going to happen to her soon: "I am going to die." In a month she was gone. Something was preparing the mother and the child for her transition into the next episode of life. The spiritual beliefs and practices of their Mormon faith helped them through this normally difficult period. No one likes to lose a healthy, intelligent child. God-centered individuals do have access to a profound sense of peace. Peace can be accessed in the midst of any trials that Life deals us.

The seven-year-old had a close cousin the same age. I'll call her Gwen. Gwen was devastated by her cousin's death. Her parents did not provide spiritual support or teaching for their young daughter. After two weeks of heavy grieving, Gwen had a pivotal experience that opened her spiritual awareness. Her deceased cousin came to her in a dream—a wonderful dream which gave her blessed assurance. Her cousin appeared radiant and beautiful. She told Gwen to stop crying and to be happy for her. Gwen was delighted.

How many of us can remember our dreams without deliberately recalling them when we wake up? What is this twilight zone between deep sleep and being awakened? What does it mean to go into the silence, to turn within? What is the secret place of the Most High? What is this initiation experience that Gwen had in a dream-like state? Was it a wake-up call?

PART III

Wake-Up Call: Initiation Experiences

At the time of initiation ceremony, after the two great
revelations there comes a moment of utter silence, and
in the interim the initiated realizes within himself the
meaning of Peace. He stands, as it were, in a void, or in
a vacuum, wherein naught seemingly can reach him; he
stands betwixt earth and heaven for a brief second, con-
cious of naught but the meaning of things as they are,
realizing his own essential divinity, and the part which
he must play when he again returns to earth service.
—Alice A. Bailey, *Initiation, Human and Solar*

SOME EXPERIENCES ARE ordinary, extraordinary, pivotal, and some experiences are introductions and in-
itiations into a new way of understanding, a *wake-up call*.
The comicstrip character is seen with a bright lightbulb
over her head. The saint is shown with a halo about fourteen inches over the head. Where do these bright ideas
come from? How do these illuminating experiences
occur?

Perhaps the most bewildering, enigmatic and arduous
task is to understand that there is a power for "Good"
in the universe that we do use and that uses us. We are

one with it. Call it what you want. The Life Force is the essential nature of all things. The Divine Spark is the awareness of essential divinity in all, as all.

This is the genesis of elucidation. All extraordinary experiences are to bring us into remembrance of our essential divinity. We have always been one with almighty God. The key words in the Bible quotes that follow are *us* and *our*:

> In the beginning was the Word, and that very Word was with God, and God was the Word . . . And the Word became Flesh and dwelt among *us* (John 1:1,14).
> And God said, "Let *us* make man in *our* image and likeness" (Genesis 1:26).

The Spirit uses the form or body as an agent to express through. We have become so enamored of the vehicle that it often takes an extraordinary experience to wake us up to Spirit. The Word is Superconsciousness. Our dilemma is our fascination with things. Our wake-up call is to know the Source, the Spirit which animates all things residing in form.

Lighthouse

The eyes are the windows of the soul. Soul represents consciousness. Our physical bodies are maintained, sustained and contained by Light. The inward gaze, acknowledgment and honor we give to Spirit shines through our eyes as disciples of Truth. Love is the fuel of the inner torch beaming through the windows of our "Lighthouse." The "True Lighthouse" cannot be contained by our physical presence. There are many ways to lighten up. What follows are some examples.

Sidney, a Black Male Nurse

I met Sidney, a thirty-five-year-old African American military nurse today. Sidney showed me many scars from injuries over most of his body. He was puzzled why he had so many scars. He had been very active most of his life, a good person not prone to fights, etc. Sidney also suffered from arthritis. He had given up strenuous sports. Coaching kids gave him satisfaction.

I gave Sidney a copy of my book *Licking Your Wounds*. While he was thumbing through the book looking for an answer to his dilemma, an intuitive flash came to me. I received an idea that was not in the book that I had given to him; a way to help the healing process came into remembrance.

"Sidney," I said, "when Spirit is expressing through the dense material body, injury and disease seem likely to come with the territory. A way that has worked for me and others is to contact the undistorted healing power residing within our spiritual being. Would you like a proactive way to use this Life Force?" He replied with an emphatic "Yes."

Healing Process

This is what I told Sidney: Find a quiet place with no distractions. Sit up or lie down. Close your eyes. Now visualize a white light like a sun approximately fourteen inches above your head. As you take in a slow, deep breath through the nose, see the light going through your body and cleansing it. See the white light and feel the breath now going beyond the physical body into the sheath we call the auric field that contains the mental and emotional bodies. Hold the breath while you repeat these words: *I have perfect assimilation, circulation and elimination.* Let the air out slowly through the mouth. Repeat this process.

It may seem strange at first, like any new exercise. It takes faith to build a new belief system. It takes understanding, love and blessed assurance to pursue a path we feel is right for us, despite what others say. A Western-trained medical doctor shared with me that he does not believe in the methods used by the Chinese doctors, such as using energy to heal cancer. We all put our faith in something and often close our minds to less costly alternatives. Yet God provides all the healing resources within Itself. The healing facilitator is a conduit, an agent, and so is the patient. There are no wrong choices or accidents.

Modern-Day Science

Western medical science at Loma Linda University Medical Center has developed a proton treatment for cancer. A proton energy beam directed to the tumor destroys it. No damage is done at the point of entry or to surrounding areas. The essence of the proton beam is precision: the high dose needed to destroy diseased tissue is concentrated in the target. Preferably, the target area is small and the problem is caught early.

The example of personal healing given to Sidney is very similar to the use of a proton beam. Using white light, or prana, to eliminate a small tumor is the same idea as the proton-beam use. There is only One Power. There is only One Mind. How we access It, how we use It, is a matter of interest. Sometimes an extraordinary event initiates us into an expanded way of knowing. Remember, the extraordinary rises out of the ashes of the ordinary. As God shows us more of Itself, we are truly blessed to know we are a necessary part of the divine unfolding. Illuminated consciousness is the "Lighthouse" that makes more lucid, more clear the pathway of the disciple of Truth. *Thou shalt guide me with thy counsel, and afterward receive me to glory* (Psalms 73:24).

As we abide in the Light of His daily teachings and walk the talk of Love, we are privileged to come home to the comfort of His all-abiding Presence. Nicole Christine describes her experiences as "The Awakening."

The Awakening

Come, my child. Come Home. Come Home. An incredibly gentle Voice called to me in my sleep . . . called with love and tenderness far surpassing the call of the most caring earthly parent awakening a beloved child. I lay serenely still without opening my eyes. The absorbing, ethereal Voice called again, *Come Home my Child. Your time is now.* The Call was but a whisper . . . a whisper so mighty no other sound dared intrude.

Slowly, I opened my eyes. It was still dark outside, but a soft-glowing light filled the trailer. Though I had spent many days and nights camping at this California spiritual retreat center, all that felt so familiar now seemed surreal.

I touched my face to see if I were real and felt tears trickling down my cheeks. Images of my two sons filled my mind and the tears flowed freely. Tears of gratitude. Of love. Of joy. Of hope for their own awakening. Suddenly, I recalled the midsummer I had become aware that I would be going Home soon and had asked that it not be before Steven's eighteenth birthday. He had turned eighteen on October 1, 1985. It was now early morning on October 6. I had been given the asked-for extension. My time was now . . .

Come. Come. Come, my child. The Voice was still calling with indescribable love and patience. I reached for my pale pink robe and slipped it on. The radiance filling the trailer brightened as I rose and stepped into my slippers. Mesmerized, I took the few steps to the trailer door. I opened it and studied the night before me. Nearby trees were illumined by the moon that played behind small puffy clouds. Familiar sounds of night creatures greeted me. I stepped onto the land I so loved. Its surface, still dusty from Indian Summer heat and dryness, had a gold-filigree look. I felt powerfully drawn to the Voice seemingly originating from the road many yards away. Lightly, I began walking along the dirt driveway. Going Home . . . Going Home . . . Going Home.

I moved with infinitesimal ease and grace. *Closer to home.* The Voice was getting fainter. The stillness stronger. Peace more powerful. Joy more encompassing. The earth dissolving more with each step I took. I felt that I was walking right out of my body and wondered if it, too, was dissolving, or if it would be found in the morning on the road in a pile, like a discarded towel dropped on the floor after a shower. I was ascending on an invisible path directly into Healing White Light. I realized I was in God's Presence. And we were walking together. I stopped walking. The Light fully surrounded me. Into the Oneness . . . Suddenly, nothing existed but Love. Pure, Pure Love. Only Love. Vibrant and encompassing Love.

I was Home! I had found my way back to our Father! Never had I felt so secure and so willing to be cared for. Please try to understand this in the depths of your being: nothing existed but Love as a constant. I did not get or give it. It is Love. IT IS LOVE. LOVE IS IT. I AM LOVE. LOVE IS I. YOU ARE LOVE. LOVE IS YOU. GOD IS LOVE. LOVE IS GOD. LOVE, *ONLY* LOVE.

Then a knowing beyond intellectualization filled me . . . knowing of our Oneness with the Father, with each other, with All That Is . . . a knowing of our Immortality . . . of our Innocence, of our Goodness, of our Beauty-filled I.

And from this state of knowing, I understood I had left "loose-ends." I wanted to be sure I did not leave the litter of my unfinished business on the planet. In the instant of that acknowledgment, I found myself again in my body with my feet on the ground. But I did not feel like a body. I did not feel a part of this world. I was Light and Love and everything about me looked and felt less dense. Everything appeared transparent.

I returned to the trailer, gliding more than walking. I looked inside. It was still aglow. I sat in the open doorway looking out into the iridescent night sky. The clouds had the same silvery radiance as the moon. The radiant clouds and moon instantly became an informational system to me. They beamed instructions down to me regarding what I needed to do to tie up my loose-ends and that I was to stay open to new information and guidance. For now, I was to return to bed for a few more hours' sleep before the coming dawn.

I felt wonderfully safe and loved as I snuggled back into my sleeping bag. As I closed my eyes, I knew I would never again forget my origin . . . who I am, who we are . . . no matter how much longer I stayed on this plane of existence.

In the days, weeks, and months ahead, I realized that Home was a state of beingness rather than a place. What is more important, I began to grasp that my awakening experience had somehow turned my attention away from the outward domain of the Father to the more inward domain of the Mother. In choosing to return Home to the Father, I began receiving the tender loving care of the Blessed Mother. The more I focused inwardly on Her Presence, the more visible She became in my outer reality.

Her boldest appearance came to me in a book, *Blessed among Women*. I became totally absorbed in the story as told by Arnold Michael, feeling a resonance I had never felt with any other version of Her life. I wrote the author expressing my deep gratitude for his work. A short time later, I received a surprising invitation to visit him and his wife, Kay, in their home.

The invitation had the same serene summoning quality I had felt that October night when the Voice called me Home. It was mid-July of the next year when I made the several hours' drive to meet the Michaels. I felt honored and a bit mystified because the note said that they rarely had guests because Arnold's health was failing.

They received me as cordially as they would a dear friend. Bishop Michael shared his vision of the Madonna Ministry. He had founded this ministry under the guidance of Mother Mary. The work of bringing forth the Divine Feminine is a task undertaken by the Madonna Ministry. The Divine Feminine was reemerging on the planet. Abruptly, he asked me if I felt called to be ordained in the Ministry. I responded with a flat and firm "No." "Please think this over," he said gently. "Now I need rest." He retired to nap and I walked about the house convinced there was nothing to think over. Called? I simply wasn't minister material.

I would like you to say "yes," my child.

I quickly turned in the direction from which the ethereally compelling Voice was coming. My eyes went directly to an astonishingly beautiful painting of Mother Mary. Her Presence filled the room and I felt as if I was having a private audience with Her. "Yes, Mother, Yes," I declared unequivocally.

I felt Her smile. She had known my answer to Her Call before I had spoken. Telepathically, I understood my ordination as an initiation. It outwardly symbolized my inward dedication to the Madonna energies and indicated I was ready to accept a more intense degree of spiritual development. As I acknowledged my readiness, I again experienced All That Is as Love, Only LOVE.

And so it came to pass, in the Year of Our Lady 1986.

I too now knew the Mother and the Father as One. I awakened to the knowing that we are all Home in the Oneness, in that Love.

Commentary

Thank you, Nicole. I would like to add that I, too, read Arnold Michael's *Blessed among Women*. It is the most moving book that I have ever read. I have read much of the sacred scriptures in the world, but nothing touches me as deeply and frequently as this story of Mary and the extended Holy Family doing God's work. Women and men have played vital roles in the origin of Christianity, each open to, and following, Divine Guidance, paving the way for Jesus to teach that the way to know the Father is *to Love*.

Arnold Michael made his earth transition on December 12, 1988, the feast day of Our Lady of Guadalupe, the patron saint of Mexico, who taught the natives to stop offering human sacrifice and reconcile themselves to God through acts of Love.

Arnold Michael also wrote a world-class novel that is currently out of print. It may some day be made into a movie, called *Brothers of the Grape*.

God Works through Love/Light/Law

The Divine Spark in us as us is most often understood as a Trinity. Mystics, metaphysicians, scientists, artists,

inventors, religionists and observers of the creative process all understand there are fundamentally three aspects
within One Life, three parts to the undifferentiated
Whole. Father, Holy Spirit Mother, and Son is an an-
thropomorphic way of knowing God. Three persons in
One God is knowing God in a microcosmic way. Knowing God as the Kingdom, Glory and Power is the mac-
rocosmic view. We can couch our terms in scientific
jargon such as energy, thought and form, or superconsciousness, subconsciousness and ordinary consciousness.

Spirit, Mind and Body, is Love/Light/Law. Another way
to say it is *Love is the Divine urge that acts through Divine Intelligence (light), which acts through Divine Law to bring Itself
into expression.* Our ignorant interpretation of the Divine
urge (will of God) is the source of all our troubles. God
as Principle is Father. God as Presence is Mother. God
as Son (child) is the expression. Let us consider how God
works through us as us a Principle and a Presence.

We Can Prove a Principle

We can prove a principle and recognize a presence. The way to
prove a Principle is to live it. Either it works or it does
not. If it works, then we know it to be true. We understand God is present in Truth. Therefore, if we live according to the most profound Principles, as we live the
Principles, we realize truths and discover God as Presence. As we live the Principles, the Divine Presence
emerges in our awareness. Since God is Omnipresent,

God is always right where we are. We move and have our being in God. Right principles are intellectually known and can be proven only by living them. Right principles always prevail over lesser ways of being in the world. Right principles are true forever. Some examples follow:

Light prevails over darkness

Love prevails over hate

Peace prevails over hostility

Joy prevails over unhappiness

Life prevails over death

Truth prevails over deceit

Realization prevails over illusion

As we live the Principles of Love, Peace and Joy, the obtuse, dense obstructions begin to dissolve, and we realize Truth as an all-pervasive Presence. An intelligent Guidance system can be accessed. As we use the Principles, we discover they work. They work to bring out the true character and attributes of God.

We do not say that darkness, hate, hostility, unhappiness, death, deceit are not experiential. We do not even call them illusions. We call them experiences. They are temporary, whereas the attributes of Life Itself are forever and can be realized. We don't make Love real. We don't make Love, Light or Truth real. These attributes of God just *are*. As we cherish these attributes, we realize what God is: an infinite beneficial Presence. We live and walk in the Spirit according to our mode of being in the world.

Ways of Being in the World

Love is the intrinsic value beyond measure. Each of us has an innate desire to express love. As we honor that desire, we honor Life Itself. How do we prove a principle? How do we prove God exists as Love? *It has to happen through us.* As we live in the Spirit of Love, our way of being in the world is for God.

If we live in the world for others, it is a more confining and troublesome way of being in the world. It invalidates our purpose for being here. We sell out, so to speak, to a lesser god. If we live in the world for self, we are egotistically bound to the things we cherish. We are pleasure-seeking, self-indulgent, manipulative and cunning. We do not know God as Principle or recognize God as Presence. We are invalidating what Spirit wants.

If we want to live in the manner of being that is intrinsic to our Godlike nature, we walk the talk. We live Love as Principle and we feel the Presence. *Love is a desire to express goodness, unconditionally. The desire to express the good makes man Christlike. Man becomes a channel through whom the love of God flows into the world,* and such a man is called a *beneficial presence,* according to Dr. Thomas Hora, who is internationally recognized for developing the teaching of Existential Metapsychiatry as well as for his book by the same title. Being here for God is the most enlightened way of being.

Confirm At-One-Ment

God does not need enlightenment. God *is* Light. God is constantly revealing Itself to self. It is our perception and understanding that is evolving. Dense energy or slow-motion energy that we call *physical* is one aspect of Divine Substance. If our mode of being in the world is for God, our energy field is focused, defined and refined. Energy raised or perhaps accelerated to the speed of light is the energy-efficient way to discover our bliss. There is no darkness in God. There is no hopelessness in real Love. It is in the holy instant, in living the Divine Principles, in seeking true fulfillment of our life's purpose that we realize and confirm at-one-ment. *No one can do it for us, it has to happen through us.*

Disease, disharmony, and discordant melodies do not exist in the mind of Superconsciousness. They are experiential, temporary, not real. What is real is the attributes of God. Why? Because they will always prevail. God does not destroy self. That is why I am a devoted advocate of getting to know God as Spirit. The form is always changing but the true Spirit is always expressing Its likeness as Love, Joy and Peace. We discover our true identity as the vibratory thoughts of our small self are in true accord with God. The sound, speed and color of light are of One substance. What are the gifts of the Spirit?

Gifts of the Spirit

A well-known attorney, gifted intellect, manufacturer of tents, and jailbird, changed his way of being in the world. He no longer lived for his religion (others, people, places or things). These things are important, but seeking first God's essential nature in one's self became his imperative. He sought the kingdom of God first. His self-importance, egotistical manner, pompous self gave way to selfless service. He learned to live first for God, the Kingdom, the Divine Principle. This person is none other than St. Paul the Apostle. Paul was a legalistic attorney who went through a mind-transforming change. His brilliant, cold intellect was softened by his spiritual realization that God is Love.

To know God we must endeavor to express wholeheartedly the fruits of the Spirit. Paul wrote, *The fruits of the Spirit are love, joy, peace, long-suffering, gentleness, goodness, faith, meekness and temperance; against such there is no law* (Galatians 5:22). Law took second seat to the fruits of the Spirit. Paul changed his way of being in the world.

Some experiences that we ordinary people are having today are like St. Paul's extraordinary awakening to Divine Guidance. Divine Guidance happens through us as us. Spirit's protection and counsel are more apparent to those that regularly practice expressing the gifts of the Spirit. Attunement to spiritual qualities heightens our spiritual sensitivity. *The Spirit itself beareth witness with our spirit, that we are the children of God* (Romans 8:16). *We are not observing a fixed reality, but a reality that is revealed or created by the act and quality of observation. Observed and observer are one. Reality is continually being co-created.* This is Heisenberg's principle, the quotation given me by the lady who shares the following extraordinary dematerialization episode.

Dematerialization Episode

This extraordinary event happened to an astute, charming lady—Frances Adams Moore. Her friends call her Fran. I am happy to be included in that group. Here is Fran's verbatim account of this life-shifting event:

> It was only after about ten years that I could talk about this experience without my voice shaking and my body shivering. Now I seem to be able to talk about it more easily.
>
> While on a leaf-viewing trip near Sheffield, Massachusetts with Caroline Grieser and Nancy Napier of the Center for Unified Living, Nancy and I looked up to see a car appear around a curve masked by tall trees—a Cadillac with a New York license plate, going very fast—a man driving and a woman in the passenger seat.
>
> The left third of the Cadillac seemed to overlap the left third of Nancy's Honda, since the road was not wide enough for two cars to pass. Nancy was driving. I was in the front passenger's seat. Caroline was in the middle of the rear seat, looking back at the charcoal shutters that we had just passed.
>
> Both Nancy and I watched the car approach so fast that there seemed to be no way to avoid a collision. My final impression was that the approaching car was less than 18 inches away from impact. I thought: This is it.

One third of Nancy's car will be sheared off, Nancy cut in half, and Caroline and I mangled.

Both Nancy and I waited for the impact, which never came. There was a total, indescribable silence. Neither Nancy nor I moved. Nancy's car never swerved. There was no sound of an engine, brakes noise, no screech of tires on gravel. It was too late for the other car to swerve around us . . . the rear end would have fishtailed into the front of Nancy's car.

We saw nothing, except a peripheral view of a brown streak. No one—Nancy, Caroline or I—heard anything. No movement of air touched the car. Our senses were incredibly alert.

Nancy exclaimed: "What happened? The cars couldn't have missed each other! Why are we still alive?" Caroline, through the rear window, could see the other car reeling down the road away from us. Nancy could see it in her rear-view mirror.

We drove on, still caught up in this incredible silence. I said, finally: "Do you suppose we've made our transition and are not yet aware of it, but have gone right on leaf-viewing?"

Nancy said: "Fran, don't say that." Then, "Should we go back and see if there is wreckage on the road?" Caroline said: "I assure you, we're still alive. I have to go to the bathroom."

Later, we decided to drive down the same road again —to "run the film through" again. We had no trouble finding the same spot again, the same house Caroline had been looking at, the same curve in the road, masked by trees.

This road is not wide enough to allow two cars to pass without both going off into the shoulder that is soft. There is a width of gravel on either side, built up into a sort of curbing. The gravel, the curbing, the shoulder were unmarked in the area. No tire tracks crossed over the gravel curbing, nor marked the soft shoulder, although all along the road there was much evidence in other areas where passing cars have both crossed over the gravel and left tracks in the shoulder.

What Happened? Why Did It Happen?

All we know is that it was a life-altering experience, and never again will I believe that anything in the physical world is solid.

Twelve Years Later

Fran writes twelve years after the event:

The uncanny silence I experienced is still very much with me at times. . . . All I know is that the description of the utter silence and the Peace, the lack of anxiety, fear, and doubt, describes my experience.

Fran also gave me a copy of Nancy's account of the life-shifting episode. Essentially, it was the same experience, including the *absolute silence*. Nancy wrote to Fran soon after the dematerialization and rematerialization episode, ''Upon reflection as I sit here recounting the experience for you, I do have to say without reservation that I feel something intervened to prevent an accident that was simply *going* to happen.''

Fran says:

I learned much from the experience, but two things I have never lost sight of were as follows:

1. Our lives are in the "hands" of a caring, loving, protective "Presence," and it is not necessary to give it a name or to label it.

2. There is nothing solid in the universe. All things are permeable.

Fran's poem relates to this experience:

> Time becomes non-time,
>   silence beyond silence reigns,
>   atoms shift in space.
>
> Wordlessly, we share
>   indefinable, yet real,
>   transfiguration.

Etheric Vitality

The creative properties that cause the impression and/or expression of materialization or dematerialization are used in science-fiction episodes. The creators of *Star Trek*, *Star Wars* and other science-fiction shows recognize that there is a way to disappear and to reappear. *Reader's Digest*, in a book entitled *Mysteries of the Unexplained*, discusses many examples of disappearance and reappearance. It is not a new phenomenon. The mastery that led to dematerialization and rematerialization can be approached best by studying the four primary functions of etheric vitality.

Students of Truth gradually become initiates in the extraordinary consciousness, i.e. they enter into superconscious levels of self-awareness. The best description of how etheric vitality works is taught by two twentieth-century sages, healers and mystics from Greece, Daskalos and Kostas. A New England professor, Kyriacos C. Markides, writes from his intimate knowledge of Daskalos and Kostas in his book *Fire in the Heart*. The professor explains how etheric vitality works:

> The functions of etheric vitality are:
> The kinetic property, which makes movement and vibration possible.
> The sensate property, which makes feelings, sentiments and sense experiences possible.
> The imprinting property, which makes the construction of thought forms and noetic images possible.
> The creative property, which makes life itself and the phenomena of materialization and dematerialization possible.

Markides says that the first three properties of etheric vitality—kinetic, sensate and imprinting—can be mastered through meditation. He gives examples of meditation in his writings. He says the fourth property, the creative property of etheric vitality, comes within the province of the Holy Spirit. It will develop naturally as a consequence of the mastery of the other three properties (i.e. kinetic, sensate, and imprinting).

The Common Ingredient

One common ingredient is the regular practice of meditation. Most people who shared their extraordinary experiences in this book understand that Spirit works through us, as us. Most practice meditation, and some consciously use etheric vitality, in a beneficial way, for the universal good.

We use outer-oriented consciousness to meet the demands of our daily activity. The true value of meditation is that it establishes a rapport with the spirit within us. The Holy Spirit as a metaphor descends upon us as we prepare ourselves to receive It. In reality the Holy Spirit's inner guidance function is everywhere. We access It from within ourselves. Through the meditative use of etheric vitality properties, we become more prepared and aware of guidance.

Etheric vitality is everywhere. It is the Life Force. Shirley MacLaine, the actress, calls it *creative energy*. During an interview on *Reflections on the Silver Screen*, Shirley said, in effect, that all energy is mental, emotional or sexual. Creating energy and using it on the screen made it easy for her to understand the use of applied metaphysics. Shirley not only practices meditation, she also teaches it. My wife, Bobbe, took a friend to one of Shirley's seminars. The practice of meditation was a very powerful experience for both of them.

Metaphysics, or that which is usually invisible, deals with apparitions, phantoms, ghosts, etc.

Ghost

I am reminded of the time I tried to sleep in a church built as a pyramid over a graveyard. All night long I sensed ghostlike beings and heard the doors and windows rattle without the benefit of wind. It took a great deal of prayer work for me to maintain a sense of assurance and a feeling of protection.

When I mentioned this ghostlike experience in church to the general congregation, I received different reactions. The minister was disappointed that I had brought up the subject. She desired to teach spiritual principles that preclude or avoid ghostly apparitions. One elderly lady was grateful I brought the subject up. She said for most of her life her ghostly experiences were invalidated by those who have not had such experiences. She learned to keep quiet regarding such matters.

I was happy to share these extraordinary events. I feel obliged to bring light where there is darkness. Even a small flashlight can give a sense of assurance to a student of Truth. Who are we to deny or judge another's experiences? It sure is nice to have someone confirm our experience, to validate our truth.

Looking for Validation

One day at the healing temple in Mexico, I was seriously wondering if I should give up administering the sacrament of laying-on-of-hands. The Holy Spirit was very active in my awareness during times of celebrating Holy Communion. I was becoming less interested in laying hands on people. I thought people often seemed so passive in their own healing process. They wanted a quick fix, like taking a drug, rather than getting to the real cause.

In my opinion, correcting the problem at the source is important. A physical problem usually has a mental and emotional derivation. Thoughts are things. Things which are thought-produced are called elementals. Are my thoughts, the elements of my creative thinking, in harmony with the Holy Spirit? Is it true that God put us here to serve one another? I wanted to know if I should continue to serve in this way. God gives us the freedom of choice as well as the answers. My answer arrived unexpectedly.

Answer Came in Unexpected Way

During the afternoon-siesta time in Mexicali, I walked the dirt streets. The sheer creativity at work in the fabrication of homes drew my attention. Casa after casa used any materials they could afford. Building codes seemed nonexistent. People took pride in having their own home. They are not poor in spirit. My mind turned back to my problem. In the poverty of my own mind, I still pondered this question: Should I cease doing laying-on-of-hands healing work? Should I continue this practice? I was hoping for some intuitive insight. Nothing came. My interest was waning in contact healing. I wanted people to learn what I had learned. We can assist the healing process through meditation, Spiritual Mind Treatment, affirmative prayer.

When I returned to the healing-temple grounds, I heard Reverend Margarita's call through the screen door: "Carlos, there is a man lying down in the temple. Put your hands on him, please." This came as a surprise. Healing work was always done in the morning.

After I completed the treatment I asked Reverend Margarita, "Why did you call me to do laying-on-of-hands work?" She replied, "I saw the Christ light above your head. That told me."

I received my answer.

I had failed to recognize something important. We are all interconnected, there is no such thing as spiritual independence. God depends on each of us to become channels for the Holy Spirit. Margarita sees things not obvious to ordinary vision. She is like Daskalos and Kostas, the Greek sages and healers. Through meditation, prayer and loving service, the teacher of Truth establishes rapport with the Holy Spirit. When the Holy Spirit and teacher act in accord, all heaven breaks loose. Etheric vitality does wonderful things in the world. The etheric vitality positively used creates miracles. We are acting in accord with the Holy Spirit.

Elementals

Elementals are thought forms. Thought forms can be positive or negative. These elementals are projections of our thoughts and feelings. Projected elementals have a life independent of the mind that created them. A curse or a blessing is a thought form. We are always creating elementals. This is why actors like Shirley MacLaine can project an image of a desired personality on the movie screen. The Life Force, or creative use of etheric vitality, takes on the life we give it.

Olga N. Worrall is without a doubt one of the twentieth century's extraordinary healers. Her expanded use of mind, or etheric vitality, is widely known. It was my privilege to meet with her on several occasions. She is small in stature and large in accomplishments. The Congress of the United States asked her to teach the medical professions what she knows.

Here is one of the things she taught me. As you know, I had lost interest in doing laying-on-of-hands work. Now healing work uses elementals to restore the remembrance of wellness. As healing facilitators we often will feel a rush of energy move through us as we do the work. The feeling of rushed energy had waned. I wondered if the gift of healing had departed. Olga reassured me that one does not need to feel the rush. It is through good intentions, faith in wellness, that the Holy Spirit does the work. God empowers us. We use the etheric vitality. How we use it is up to us.

Constructive Use of Etheric Vitality

Olga and her equally famous husband, Ambrose, never charged for healing work. He was a successful aerospace engineer. Ambrose was able to use his intuitive faculties in concert with his analytical, reasoning mind. Ambrose used his elementals well to serve humanity. Olga's use of etheric vitality was deliberate and beneficial. Her talents were studied by many universities and organizations. I first met her at a healing symposium in Los Angeles. Olga told us of one university's repeated experiment. They would take two flats of identical plants. One flat they labeled A, the other labeled B. Each week they called Olga at an agreed time. She then directed creative, loving elementals to flat A, and not to flat B, through the power of affirmative prayer.

The creative etheric has no choice but to use what our mind and emotions conjure. The vital, sincere elementals helped flat A plants flourish. Within three months, flat A plants had more than twice the rate of growth over flat B. They were healthy, strong and more vigorous. This experiment and others like it were repeated with the same results. Olga has also won awards for flowers from her garden. Her constructive, loving use of mind caused positive results in the form of healthy, larger, beautiful plants.

Elementals and the Law of Attraction

Elementals, like birds of a feather, flock together. Loving, kind, constructive, joyful, happy thoughts will attract more of the same. Angry, hurtful, destructive thoughts are akin to more of the same. Negative elementals are often caused by our being too possessive: "Don't mess with our religion, our country, our family, our property, and our money."

We often take the things we cherish too seriously. We fail to recognize that the law of attraction is more than an abstract idea. Some of us understand the law and use it to better our circumstances and to help others, such as Olga and Ambrose Worral. Some use it unwittingly, ignorantly or foolishly. Nevertheless, what we put into the law repeatedly will come home to roost.

Sometimes we learn the hard way, through suffering. Such is the case of the man possessed by negative elementals.

Man Possessed

I received a call from a distressed mother. Her son, James, who is in his late twenties, was thrown in a local southern California jail for a minor offense. Apparently, James abused himself through the use of drugs. His mother's chief concern was his very noticeable change in personality. She knew it was more than a minor alteration brought on by drug usage.

The mother I'll call Carol. Carol suspected that James was possessed. Intuitively, I felt she was correct in her diagnosis. Carol knew I had some experience with exorcisms and thought I could be of help. I had some training with a master teacher, Reverend Margarita. She had taught me to do hands-on-exorcism with real cases in Mexico. It took me a while to break through my stubborn reluctance to accept that cases of possession exist. They are more than ancient myths or distorted movie fantasies. Healing facilitators need to be knowledgeable and well prepared spiritually. To be an effective channel for the Holy Spirit, we must be free from our own agenda and possessive tendencies.

> Possessions, be it by a demon, an elemental, or departed human, can take place only if there are reasons: that is, when the individual vibrates analogously with whoever or whatever tries to enter him. In other words, the person must himself have the predisposition to hurt.

This is the nature of possession according to master teacher Daskalos in the excellent book *The Magus of Strovolos*, by Kyriacos C. Markides. It is easy to understand that what we give out comes back to haunt us with undaunted certainty.

This lifetime is not of sufficient duration to appreciate the accumulation of karmic debt that is attributed to our present circumstances. In the immediate present we have the opportunity to use the etheric vitality to create constructive changes.

A Tale of Absentee Exorcism

I told Carol I was not interested in driving to some far-off jailhouse to visit her son, James. Carol told me that she had confronted James with her idea of possession. He thought his Mom was "off the wall." Possession did not fit James' description of himself or even enter into his awareness. "Carol," I said, "I have no experience in doing absentee exorcism. Here is the name and address of a colleague, Reverend Maurey. Perhaps you can get his Chicago telephone number from the operator. He can help you. Reverend Eugene Maurey has written a book on the subject of absentee exorcisms."

Several days later the phone rang. It was Carol. She had not reached Reverend Maurey. She requested my assistance. This time my intuitive light went on. Healing is no problem for the Holy Spirit. *I* do not do healing; *God* does. So I informed Carol that I would immediately take the situation into prayer treatment. Treatment is a specific type of prayer designed to meet the challenge of exorcism.

A week later Carol called me. She was most cheerful, a welcome change from her earlier parental concern about her son. Carol told me that her son's girlfriend visited him at his new place of incarceration, the Los Angeles County Jail. "James was a changed person," she said. Here is what James' girlfriend reported:

James was sitting in his new cell. Two guards walked by his cell with Richard Ramirez, the infamous nightstalker. Ramirez' eyes were dark and flashing a red glow as he stared directly into James' eyes. As Ramirez spoke the words "thank you" to James, James felt a tremendous release. Something left him and went into Ramirez. "Maybe my mother was right. Somehow I was possessed."

"Thank God," I said to Carol. "Be sure you advise your son to change his ways or chances are whatever possessed him will come back stronger." The elementals were transferred from James to Ramirez. The Law of attraction works like a magnet drawn to metal. Prayer treatment gave James a reprieve, an opportunity to change his thoughts and create beneficial thought forms. Ramirez' interest in killing, stalking and destructiveness attracted the negative elementals into his auric field.

Some things like the story of absentee healing may be difficult to believe for the person that is a linear-thinking materialist or a rigid orthodox rationalist. Nothing is going to change their point of view. We all can get stubborn and close-minded. Only the power of love can break down the crystallization of limited thinking.

Complementary healing facilitators often deal with problems that orthodox methodologies don't understand or don't want to understand. Life is multidimensional, holodynamic, and to appreciate the Allness of Spirit, we integrate all possibilities. Love is the dynamic that moves us into action, and Intelligence is the application of love with pure intention to serve.

Here is some insight into the heart of a healing facilitator—my colleague Eugene Maurey, who shares this story he titled, "You, the Healer."

You, the Healer

We who are healers, Spiritual Healers, Reiki Healers, Psychic Healers or by whatever name we wish to be called, have a kinship with one another in the desire to heal. We ask ourselves: why do we have this desire? Did it arise through curiosity or to assuage our ego? Could it have been brought about by our desire to help someone who had a specific problem? Do we consider ourselves born healers? On the surface it may appear that any of the above brought on this desire. I don't think so.

As you progressed in the path as a healer, not everything seemed to go as you would like or expected. You found to be a healer was hard work with long hours, often with little or no recognition or appreciation. Few of you are given adequate remuneration for the effort you make, and all too frequently you are not even compensated for your out-of-pocket expenses. So often when you have given a successful healing, the patient simply thinks that it would have happened anyway, and never thinks to say, "Thank you." When it comes to feedback to measure the effectiveness of your effort, you can dismiss it; you will rarely hear a word. Oh yes, you will hear from a satisfied patient who has an uncle with an incurable disease, lying in a hospital, a few days from death. And would you give him healing? Why in the world does anyone want to be a healer! I'll tell you why. You CARE.

Let's talk about this word *care*. Your heart goes out to the sufferer. You have been given this blessing to be a healer and you simply cannot stand by without trying to help. You have compassion, you care; you stop whatever you are doing and give your full attention to the patient. We know that we have little control of this Power we use; the healing may occur or it may not: a greater Intelligence determines the outcome. Let me tell you of several unusual healings in which I participated.

Some years ago, I visited a dear friend in a hospital. Nearby I could hear a dreadful moan. I investigated and peeked into the adjacent room. On what appeared to be a flat bed lay an ancient woman, emaciated with her bones clearly visible through her paper-thin skin. At intervals of ten seconds she would raise her head slightly and utter a most mournful moan. There was no question what I had to do. I promptly gave her healing. The results were out of my hands and I accepted it. That night the lady was relieved of her pain and passed on. For me, this was a successful healing.

As an exorcist I have witnessed some extraordinary healings. Let me summarize one case of a seriously ill young woman who at the age of twenty-six had a series of operations and, when I was told about her, was scheduled for another. I found that the lady was spirit-possessed by a single entity. As a dowser, using my pendulum, I asked questions to determine who the entity could possibly be. It proved to be her mother who had died when the girl was eleven. The exorcism was a simple one. I asked the spirit mother to sit down beside me (I could not see her but assumed that she was present) and I explained to her that although she loved her daughter by being with her, she was causing the illness that the daughter was experiencing. Actually, she was bringing to her child the disease that had caused her own death. Furthermore, I explained that the girl had but six months to live. I concluded by giving the mother the option to stay with her daughter or leave. She left. The daughter canceled the scheduled operation and in the years that followed experienced excellent health.

Permit me to tell of another rather extraordinary case. I was told by a woman that her husband in Poland had a stroke and for the past three days lay in a hospital paralyzed on one side of his body. I offered to give him healing. The woman had never heard of such healing but, having little choice, said, "Please do." I closed my eyes and imagined a white light enveloping the man who I presumed was lying on a hospital bed. I equated the light with the power of the healing force. My concentration was such that I unintentionally drifted off to sleep. Awakening, I felt that the healing was a good one. The next day the man in Poland walked out of the hospital!

Yes, we who are healers care for those in distress around us. I wonder if there is a difference between the word *care* and the word *love*. I don't think so.

PART IV

Go to the Source: Divine Guidance

A great river may have many tributaries and you can find
this main stream by following any of the tributaries back
to its point of origin. So it is that the senses perceive many
things that appear different and separate but actually
arise from a common source. When you are able to perceive that you too have come from, are sustained by, and
return to this source, you realize your supreme identity.
The river of your individual self merges with the ocean
of Universal Mind and Yoga is achieved!

THANK YOU, RICHARD HITTLEMAN, for this profound
teaching in your book *Guide to Yoga Meditation*.

Years ago, when I was working in the mainstream of
the insurance industry, I was innocently practicing Yoga
meditation with Richard Hittleman and his two attractive female helpers. It was a wonderful way to start the
day in a relaxed way. I spread out a towel in front of the
TV set in my bedroom and practiced these wonderful
stretching exercises which were on the public broadcast-
ing system. The family knew not to disturb me during
this thirty-minute period.

Sometimes we really know when we are in our right

place. I was enthusiastic about what I was doing in the insurance industry. I had a well-balanced life between business, family and civic duties. Each day I exercised, played, prayed, worked, ate and drank in moderation. I earnestly practiced the Judaic-Christian principles I had learned. I always felt ''good'' when I was doing good. I would feel badly if I violated the sacred trust to do ''good.''

''Do-Gooders''

Many souls fail to find God because they want a religion which will remake society without remaking themselves, according to Fulton J. Sheen. Sometimes we, as do-gooders, are filled with righteous indignation. We are more interested in finding fault than in finding the solution—love offers. If we feel angry or blind with rage it is merely an invitation to go back to the Source. It is called *practicing the Presence*. Hatha Yoga is a wonderful tool. Prayer is a wonderful tool. Genuine gratitude and practicing the Principles are daily devices to bring us into attunement with transcendental realization. Daily practice is vital to our spiritual growth. To become good at anything requires interest and practice. To be here for God requires interest and practice, don't you agree?

As do-gooders we are *superficially* here for God. We are more interested in *looking good* than in *being good*. The will-to-good requires knowing the Source. Practicing the Presence is God realization. What can God do through us in this holy instant? God is all-powerful and everywhere present. God can show us that the essence of Itself is Peace even in the midst of conflicting values. Peace brings to the table a workable solution whereas anger has no loving resolution.

Conflicting Values

I received a call from my brother-in-law. He was beside himself. We did not get along, yet he was calling to ask my help. He did not know the whereabouts of his wife or four children. He thought I might have a clue. They were missing and left no obvious clues to their disappearance. So I agreed to meet with him the following day.

I arrived early and no one was home. A neighbor recognized me and told me that my sister left with her children to live with her mom in the state of Washington. My brother-in-law had been in jail for three days. He was charged with child assault and molestation of his own children. He was released on bail until the case was decided.

Red flags went up. Righteous indignation took hold. I felt justified in retaliation. I had always thought I could justifiably take another's life for raping or deliberately inflicting major harm to any member of my family. The hero that I identified with in the movies gave me permission to become the transgressor, once transgressed. Thank God my brother-in-law had not arrived early.

I decided that I'd better leave the premises and sort out

this information calmly. I went home and refused to take calls from my brother-in-law. After much persistence, I did take a call from him and agreed to meet him on my turf. We met the next day after hours at my insurance office.

I met with a depressed man. He met with one confused insurance proprietor. My values were in conflict. My heroic value system justified retaliation. My spiritual value system guided me to calm down for three hours. Much to my wife's dismay, who had wanted me home to dinner two hours earlier, I sat listening to him for another hour. This greatly distraught man described his recent sad tale. He thought of himself as victimized by his two daughters' untruths. I found his tale hard to believe.

Something extraordinary happened as I suspended judgment and listened. I became clear and realized that an inner calm and love prevailed over the grey confusion. I got up from my desk, hugged and reassured him things would work out. Some of his depression lifted, and I felt at peace as I said goodnight and we parted.

Twenty years later most of the wounds are healed. My sister, her ex-spouse, and her children all found different support systems that taught spiritual values. Some turned to Mormonism, Christian fundamentalism, Charismatic Catholicism and Buddhism. You can go back and reread in Part I, subtitled "How to Grow Spiritually," and see how my niece Elaina changed dramatically.

Nothing Happens by Accident

By my worldly values, I can deliberately and justifiably inflict harm for any reason that validates my aggressive behavior, like the old adage which condones "an eye for an eye and a tooth for a tooth." Such foolish beliefs can lead us into a toothless and blind society. It does not take a genius to realize that retribution begets retribution. Nothing happens by accident. We become what we cherish and believe.

My Source had inspired me, and I responded to It. My individual stream of consciousness became aware of Universal Source. God is Peace. My dedication to biblical principles taught me love. My recent practice of Hatha yoga taught me union with the One. My growing appreciation for the philosophy of Science of Mind taught me the value of an affirmative prayer. Like attracts like.

What is our purpose for being in the world? Is it for self, for others, for God? If we are here for God, what is our belief about God? If you have read this far, you believe something Benevolent guides us home. Yet, like a wandering tributary, though we venture afar, go astray, we never can be separated from our Source.

Free to Choose

How we come to know, to love and to serve God is our choice. How our Source guides us is Her choice, His choice, or Its choice. Call God what you may—the All-Pervasive Nameless One, in which all move and have their being. When we have strayed from the will-to-good, we need to remember God. We are free to choose, but not free from the consequences of our choices. Such is the Law. *Let him who wishes to be near God abandon all that alienates him from God* (Harith Ibn Asad Al-Muhasibi, 7th century).

Does God Use Intermediaries in Guidance?

When we say God uses intermediaries to do His work, what are we really saying? Simply this: God uses all aspects of Itself to help us remember. *The quest of man for God, which becomes in the end the most ardent and enthralling of all his quests, begins with the first vague questioning of Nature and a sense of something unseen both in himself and her* (Sri Aurobindo, *The Life Divine*).

God overlooks nothing and realizes everything that is eternally true. What we call the dark side of the force is the unenlightened way of living. It inevitably leads to suffering. No darkness exists in God. That is the eternal truth of Being. Our spirit resides, moves and has its being in the eternal One. We have simply turned away from the light. We are holding on to unenlightened beliefs that are not spiritually sound. This point was very vividly driven home to me by some healing work I did for a young woman I'll call Nancy. Nancy wore thick lenses to correct her physical sight. As I put my hands over her eyes I asked Nancy and her cousin to join me in prayer.

After I took my hands off Nancy's eyes a few minutes later, she could see perfectly well without her glasses. Her perfect vision lasted just a brief moment. In our counseling session later, it became apparent to me that Nancy was not ready to release deceit with a few key people in her life. The deceitful web involved her female married cousin. Both of them were having an affair with the same man. An amoral man who thought he was God's gift to women, he had no regard for marriage or responsibilities for parenting, even though he was a licensed marriage and family counselor. Nancy deceitfully lured this man away from her cousin, who was married. She engaged the male counselor in romantic sexual exchange. Nancy pretended to use contraceptives. She got pregnant. Her intent to have the man "make an honest woman of her" failed. She sued the counselor for his amoral behavior and threatened to have his counseling license revoked if he would not marry her.

True love is full of compassion and free of lies. Nancy hated other people for lying to her. She was unwilling to look at herself honestly. Nancy felt hate for people who did not speak the truth. Hate blinds us from noticing the truth. Compassion is nonjudgmental 20/20 spiritual vision.

Deceit cannot invalidate truth. Truth *is*. If we repeatedly hold on to something we believe negates the Truth, it will show up in our physical, emotional or mental bodies as a reflection of our darkened consciousness. We can feel or sense the light or dark use of the force when we walk into a room. Some churches, temples or sacred sites glow, and it can be seen by those who read auric fields. We can walk into a room where a recent fight occurred and sense the hostility in the atmosphere.

The Life Force cannot be dark in a real sense. God is Light, Love and Truth. In Truth, the eternal essence cannot be distorted. *Thoughts are things* serves as a basis for psychosomatic psychology. Biofeedback teaches what we think makes a noticeable difference in the quality of our health. We can think and feel less than Truth. This dichotomy is not real in the Mind of God. God knows Truth for what it is, not for what it seems to be.

Truth Cannot Be Invalidated

When we feel separated from our Source, we are living in an unenlightened way. Life or Truth is not absent. Life as Truth is the perpetual Allness of God constantly animating Itself in form. What is termed the "Light side of the Force" is simply the realization of God as Love and Light. What is termed as the "dark side of the force"? The dark side means we have turned our attention from spiritual values or we are ignorant of them. We have become too interested in temporal things. Simply put: we are ignoring the spiritual Truth of being in the world for God. *Know God, and all fetters will be loosed. Ignorance will vanish. Birth, death, and rebirth will be no more. Meditate upon Him and transcend physical consciousness. Thus will you reach union with the Lord of the universe* (Svetasvatara Upanishad, prior to 400 B.C.)

Invisible Presence

Since time immemorial, and probably before time and space, we, in our Spirit bodies, have been aware of invisible forces. Forces are at work behind the fabric of physical reality. Every creative idea, every inspiring thought, every invention and contraption comes through the invisible presence of Life Itself. Mr. Nobel invented dynamite. Dynamite's potential always existed in Divine Mind. Nobel simply discovered the idea and used it. It is interesting to note, Mr. Nobel was also a pacifist. Dynamite has peaceful uses, like clearing away rock and earth for building dams, tunnels, mines, etc. The royalties and profits from his many nineteenth-century inventions, support the Nobel prizes of science, literature and peace today. *What is, is in God, and nothing can exist or be conceived without God*, according to Baruch Spinoza.

Intermediaries

I have come to the stage of realization in which I see that God is walking in every human form and manifesting Himself alike in the sage and in the sinner, stated Sri Ramakrishna. Of course, Jesus of Nazareth knew and taught us to love our enemies and those who spitefully use us. Those who express unconditional Love have no need of an intermediary. God is Love. *We affirm that man is the embodiment of the Divine, and that every human being, containing within himself something of God, is of infinite moral worth, too sacred to be exploited or oppressed* (Israel Goldstein, *A Book of Jewish Thoughts*).

God exists in intermediaries. Moses was an extraordinary mediator. *And the Lord said unto Moses, Thus thou shalt say unto the children of Israel, Ye have seen that I have talked with you from heaven* (Exodus 20:22). An invisible Presence gave Moses laws and rules which, if followed, would bring individuals closer to the resemblance of God.

At a later stage in the development of humankind Jesus of Nazareth came as a mediator. Jesus demonstrated the greatest example of Love. He taught and lived it. He fulfilled the law of being that God gave to Moses. "Love God and love one another."

Jesus, in fulfilling the law, discovered the resemblance of God within Himself. That is why He is called the true Son of God. Jesus' love and light were so great he was later called Christ. Christos is the light of God. Jesus' brother James put it this way in a letter: *Every good gift and every perfect gift is from above, and cometh down from the Father of lights, with whom is no variableness, neither shadow of turning* (James 1:17). The Principles are the gifts. Living the Principles restores our spiritual integrity, bringing us into a keener sense of living in the Presence. This is extraordinary insight from James, an ordinary brother of an extraordinary individual.

James had an extraordinary understanding of God as

being all-beneficent. I feel we have been misled by some intermediaries translating "the word." James helped me clarify the dichotomy of a vengeful God and a God of Love. A God of Love does not lead us into temptation; this is a misunderstanding, from my perspective. Temptation is of our own doing. God is so liberal with us, yet our freedom is a two-edged sword. As spiritual beings we are licensed, so to speak, to express *truth* freely. Anything less than *truth* has undesirable consequences.

I have had difficulty with the mistranslated words of Matthew in what is commonly accepted as The Lord's Prayer. *Lead us not into temptation,* if properly translated, says, *And do not let us enter into temptation.* This correction is found in the Aramaic translation by George M. Lamsa. Jesus' spoken language was Aramaic.

James, I like your style; I wish I knew you better. I agree wholeheartedly with you when you write, *Let no man say when he is tempted, I am tempted of God: for God cannot be tempted with evil, neither tempteth he any man: But every man is tempted, when he is drawn away of his own lust, and enticed* (James 1:13,14). Now I can relate to James' teaching. Perhaps he is helping me understand from the "other side."

Invisible Made Visible

What can be said? Many people throughout all ages are helped by invisible beings, guardian angels, saints and sages. The invisible realms are less dense and coexist with our world. Our subconscious minds are not unconscious of such realities. We are one with God in Spirit, and Spirit is everywhere present. We can access any individualization of the Whole. The whole is contained in the Universal Mind.

> We all look forward to the day when science and religion shall walk hand in hand through the visible to the invisible. Science knows nothing of opinion, but recognizes a government of law whose principles are universal. . . . Revelation must keep faith with reason, and religion with law—while intuition is ever spreading its wings for greater flights—and science must justify faith in the invisible.
>
> —Ernest Holmes (*The Science of Mind*)

Within the invisible realm is a psychic sea. Thoughts are things and they are never lost. The mortal mind is simply a reflection from the mental sea of accumulated thought forms. How often I observe my little thoughts arguing, finding fault, creating conflict. This is an invitation to "change the channel." We are receiving mirrorlike impressions from the microwave satellites focused on less than the will-to-good. These thought forms are the products of unenlightened thinking and are distortions of Truth.

As students of Truth, we are attempting to seek the resemblance of God. We are trying to become less interested in our mortal mind and more interested in Divine Mind. As we succeed, everything and everyone becomes part of the Guidance System. *We are all strings in the concert of His joy; the spirit from His mouth strikes the note*

and tune of our strings (Jakob Boehme). In the concert of
His joy our spiritual body glows.

Light Body

The light body is refined, a spiritually cellular light body
made in the fabric of the Almighty. It is less dense than
what we call our physical bodies. As we use our mortal
minds to express the will-to-good, our mental, emotional
and physical bodies are intuitively filled with light. Our
aspiration and inspiration have met and unity is recognized. Our mortal minds are transformed. They are
redeemed in the Spirit. Our light-body, sometimes called
astral body, glows with the pristine assurance that we are
being here for God. Our light is no longer being hidden
within the dense physical form. As St. James said, *Every
Good gift and every perfect gift is from above, and cometh down
from the Father of lights, with whom is no variableness, neither
shadow of turning* (James 1:17). This is the astral or light-
body that does not know illness, disease or separation
from God. It knows perfect Peace, unconditional Love
and boundless Intelligence, which reside in the Father of
lights.

Know Thy Job

Job is a wonderful Bible story. Job is a name spelled the
same as the noun *job*: meaning a piece of work. Although
it is pronounced a little differently, it is the workable

model of being here for God and living in the world. Job worked the spiritual principles and lived in the Presence. He is the central figure in an Old Testament parable of the righteous sufferer. You might ask yourself, "Who wants to suffer, for Heaven's sake?" On the other hand, who escapes the problems arising from the karmic sea of unenlightened living?

Job is a book of the Bible bearing his name. He is most likely a mythological character produced by a divinely inspired playwright. He is a model of being here for God. Despite the ups and downs, the adversities, suffering, misfortunes and famine that he experienced, Job held fast to spiritually workable principles. Job penetrated the temporal of the physical plane and paid little attention to the distractions of the unenlightened use of mortal mind.

Behind all temporal things is the light-body that knows. Job acknowledged God's omnipresence when he instructed his friends to open their heart to discover God. Sincere seekers of Truth can find God now. *But ask now the beasts, and they shall teach you; and the fowls of the air, and they shall tell you. Or speak to the earth, and it shall teach you; and the fishes of the sea shall declare to you* (Job 12:7,8). Divine Guidance is available now. Guidance is everywhere, and is available to everyone and everything.

Divine Guidance

Perhaps the most difficult idea to understand is that we are spiritual beings living in the world, but not of it. How is that possible? Jesus said of his disciples in Truth, *They*

are not of the world, even as I am not of the world (John 17:16).
What did he mean? He meant that everything that is
"Good," everything that is worthwhile, is acceptable to
"Him that sent me." This goodness is found in our spirit
or astral body that knows God. The temporal body or
physical form is like an astral projection or hologram. We
think we are the astral projection or holographic movies
on the screen of life. In reality we are the light bulb that
never burns out. As we turn our attention to spiritual
Principles, our wattage goes up. Our individual projec-
tor gives a more realistic animation of what God is. Vir-
tual reality can not deny the truth of our spiritual being.

Jesus told his disciples of Truth: *Be of good cheer; I have
overcome the world* (John 16:33). *Yet a little while, and the
world seeth me no more; but you see me: Because I live, ye shall
live also. At that day ye shall know that I am in my Father, and
ye in me, and I in you* (John 14:19,20). In the astral or light-
body, we are made in the image and likeness of God.
This point is shown in a vision.

Vision with a Message

I was maintaining a small apartment near the church
where I worked four days a week. I was teaching classes
on the science of understanding how God works through
us. Late one evening I received a long-distance call from
a friend, Dawn. What she had to share with me brought
tears to my eyes. It also brought a warm glow to my
body. Here is what she told me:

"I was sitting in my living room one night around

11:00 P.M. The family had gone to bed. I just had fallen into a light sleep when I received a vision." I asked her, "Was it like a dream?" "No," she replied. "It was a vision. I was alert, not asleep. I had been worrying about my mother, who had been stricken with Alzheimer's disease. My relationship with my mother had not been very good, and I have some regrets for not resolving these ill feelings. How could I let her know I love her? She can't remember who I am. This was my dilemma."

Here is the part of the conversation where my intuition lit up. I asked her, "What about the vision?" She could hardly wait to tell me about it. It became obvious she needed to give me the background first.

In Dawn's vision her mother, who has Alzheimer's disease, appeared in a temporal, physical body and in her astral body. Behind and above this dual image appeared Mary, a radiant divine Mother.

Temporal Body

The mother is lost in her diseased impression of what we call her temporal, physical body. She has forgotten her Source. Her clogged memory is saturated with earthly values. The Psychic Sea of mental thought forms is filled with less than whole, perfect and complete mental thoughts. These thoughts fall short of fulfilling what God wants.

Astral Body

This image of her was fully alive, well and aware. The astral body image is whole, perfect and complete. It is an individual resemblance of God in the microcosm. Her spirit or soul body is her radiant body known by God to be of Itself. This light-body cannot be destroyed. However, it does put on the appearance or garment of an earth-bound being shrouded in the mystery of a temporal world.

World Mother

Dawn's vision includes a third image, an image of an infinite Mother, a beatific vision of the Virgin Mary. She is radiating the resemblance of pure, unconditional love—a pure emanation of what God is as an immaculate Mother; Love itself, shining Its resemblance of a spiritually complete embodiment to Dawn's mother's soul or astral body. The mystery of the triune image of God revealed Itself to Dawn. The physical body is a hologram, a sort of space vehicle, a physiological expression. This third or outer body is here for our learning.

The Source, the astral body, the physical-like-form, Is-Ra-El, Mind-Body-Spirit, Father–Son–Holy Spirit, Brahman-Vishnu-Shiva are ways of describing how the triune Spirit of God works through us.

The Message

The basic message to Dawn was for her not to worry. What I received from her vision is the following list of *Don'ts* and one *Do*.

Don't *judge the form by appearance.*

Don't *judge the misguided ways of being in the world in ourselves and others.*

Don't *take the sins or mistakes of ourselves or parents too seriously.*

Don't *take one anxious moment over things in the world.*

Don't *repeat the mistakes of generations past.*

Do *seek the resemblance of God.*

Ten years later I met Dawn for breakfast. She told me she is able to see the spirit body of people. This body is perfect. Dawn not only believes it is true, she actually knows it is true. This expanded awareness helps her help others. She is a good friend and counselor to many in the clergy.

Our astral body is like an individual unit of awareness. If our focus is on the lower use of mortal mind, we have a restless confused mind. We have amnesia. We are lost. Our way of being in the world is for self or for others. We are like Jacob, who had struggled and made worldly values more important than spiritual values. Through the grace of God, Jacob turned his attention, his unit of awareness, to an enlightened, empowered way of being in the world. *Let every soul be subject unto the higher powers. For there is no power but of God: The powers that be ordained of God* (Romans 13:1). The Divine Mother represents the Christ, the higher use of the powers.

Love God and love one another is a simple rule. But it takes an extraordinary commitment to practice this rule. It is through devotion to Spirit that we are transformed as St. Paul said—*by the renewing of our minds.* We become more sensitive to the invisible means of support that are here for us. Even in the temporal Alzheimer's-diseased body, as well as the astral body, there is resident the divine Father/Mother.

Solution

When the astral body, or our individual unit of awareness, turns its attention to and lives the Divine Principle, a wonderful and extraordinary transformation takes place. There is a growing awareness of the invisible "helping hands" that Joseph Campbell, author and teacher extraordinaire, would recognize within himself. In *The Inner Reaches of Outer Space*, one of his many books, he says, *Moreover, compassion, as we learn from* The Tibetan Book of the Dead, *is of two orders: compassion with, and compassion without, attachments. The latter is of Buddha and conduces to enlightenment, whereas the former leads to rebirth among the Hungry Ghosts.*

Inner Plane

The nonhungry Ghosts, or spirits that have found their fulfillment or realization in Spirit, are the seen and un-seen, known and unknown beneficent beings. These be-ings are working to bring us out of our unenlightened way of being in the world. There are many Way-showers. On the inner plane resides Divine Giving and a pure In-telligence, Infinite Mind. This unseen Guest has perma-nent residence everywhere.

All men receive some *light, and this light is always the same light. There is one nature diffused throughout all nature; One God incarnated in all peoples,* said Ernest Holmes in *The Science of Mind.* The blessings, the blessed and the blessor are One to the pure of heart. The abstract essences of Peace, Joy, Love and Abundance are most real to the students of Truth. Divine Guidance is everywhere to be found and nowhere to be seen, except by those ready to see.

The one nature, the one power, the only Life there is can be understood as expressing Itself as Spirit, Mind and Body. These three aspects of the triune nature of God are expressed everywhere—the vitality of God, the living Truth we can understand as Principles. Principles are all-pervasive thought forms in the Divine Orchestra-tion of life. When we are in accord, in resonance with the Divine Melody, we become increasingly aware of the Grand Conductor. In the human orchestration of life we have been playing many base notes out of sync with our Divine Feminine nature. We are now going through a harmonic convergence to restore our way of being in the world in a less harsh manner. The new melody is noted in the players who express the will-to-good: right human relationships and group endeavor.

We are adding grace to power, nurturance to force, intuition to rational thinking. The Divine Mother is helping us give more attention to spiritual values. Let us examine the Divine Mother and Father as being Omnipresent.

PART V

Divine Mother and Father: Principle and Presence

The Divine Mother Principle

THE DIVINE MOTHER principle has been with us since the beginning. *And Adam called his wife's name Eve; because she was the mother of all living* (Genesis 3:20). Eve's spirit is evident in the continuity of the great goddess of many names and forms. Devi, Inanna, Ishtar, Astarte, Artemis, Isis, Venus, Athena, Mary and others have given birth symbolically and metaphorically to new ages. The Divine Mother Principle resides within all of us.

Mother Mary

Something in me was delighted and surprised to hear Marianne Williamson, author of a best-selling book on the subject of Love, refer people to Mother Mary. Several mothers and school counselors were concerned about the rapidly increasing number of pre-teen girls wanting to commit suicide. Mothers and counselors looked for a solution to these very real problems. They experienced the threat and actual performance of suicide in their families and schools.

Marianne Williamson advised them: "Go to a Catholic or Episcopal church. Find an icon of Mother Mary. Ask her help."

I do not need to be convinced that Mary dwells in the "Secret Place of the Most High" with others who have found their way home. I am reminded that Mother Mary brought a profound sense of peace to a group of my acquaintance.

I was invited to give the last keynote address to an audience of International New Thought Alliance members. At the end of the address, I invited members of the audience to come forward on a volunteer basis. As they came forward, I anointed them with water. Approximately 90% of the three hundred people attending this week-long conference came forward to receive the blessing. I had recently obtained the water at the shrine where Mother Mary appeared at Lourdes, France. Many cures occur there through water she blessed.

I felt an extraordinary flow of gentle, powerful energy pass through me as I blessed each one. A profound sense of peace filled the large auditorium.

My host scheduled loud, live, peppy music as a conclusion immediately following my keynote address. The five-piece band roused no one. I understand the peace that dwells in the Father, in the Mother and in the Son. Peace is not just a name or a passing experience. Peace is an enlightened way of being in the world. Peace is more than a passing quality. Peace is an everlasting expression of Spirit. The blessed assurance of peace is resident in our spirit. Peace becomes more obvious as we habitually harmonize with the will-to-good. *A spirit united to God, in a habitual manner by prayer and charity, acquires wisdom, goodness, strength, benevolence, liberty, greatness of soul* (St. Maximus the Confessor).

We are entering a New Age where will, creativity and wisdom proclaim that competitiveness will surrender to cooperation, that aggressiveness will reduce itself to assertiveness, that reasoning will honor intuitive knowing, that inner union will demonstrate and outer cleavage to temporal things will loosen. Let Love prevail.

Let the Divine Mother archetype come forth and give birth to Christ, the enlightened Son. Let the original pattern, the astral likeness, the resemblance of God, the will-to-good, prevail.

> **archetype:** 1. the original pattern or model from which all things of the same kind are copied or on which they are based; prototype. 2. (in Jungian psychology) an inherited unconscious idea, pattern of thought, image, etc., universally present in individual psyches.

The Divine Father Principle

The mind or individual unit of awareness that is focused by the power of will is inherent in the Divine Father Principle. The will-to-Good is the seed of Abraham, the Buddha, the Tao. It is the Christlike awareness.

It takes the power of will to choose and to surrender the attachments of worldly treasures and turn over our secular aims to the higher principles. It takes will to cast aside the undesirable thought forms that arise in our mortal minds. It takes a combination of will and inner knowing to bring forth the fruits of the Spirit. It takes the will of humility to give up the pride of separation. It takes the grace of God to find the resident ''good'' in All.

Being here for God requires an understanding of the nature of God. To understand God's nature requires grace. *To receive grace we need only love its Donor* wrote Mathias Scheeben (*Glories of Divine Grace*, 1886).

''My Soul Doth Magnify the Lord''

Mary, an ordinary handmaiden, who has spent lifetimes of living the Principle and practicing the Presence, is called *Blessed art thou among women* by the angel Gabriel as reported by Luke the physician (Luke 1:28). Luke is definitely a doctor we can trust. He says that Mary said to her cousin Elizabeth, *My soul doth magnify the Lord* (Luke 1:46). These words mean Mary experienced an intensification and heightening of her ordinary Godlike awareness.

Mary said, *He has helped his servant Israel, in remembrance of his mercy* (Luke 1:54). Israel represents the enlightened way of being in the world. As we are for God, God is for us. The Truth is, God is always for us and through His mercy we can remember. The remembrance is accessed through the will-to-good, right way of being in the world; and our soul (astral body) "will magnify the Lord." Our soul is employed by Spirit. Our small, ordinary self is called into extraordinary service. *For He that is mighty is doing great things through me; and holy is His name.*

Grace and Power

If we live in God's graces, we are given His Power more abundantly. We must have an understanding of God's nature. There must be faith, acceptance and realization. We must discern the will-to-good resident in our own hearts and religiously follow its beckoning.

A musical group, well known to the world, went through a spiritual transformation. It became evident in their lyrics. They put their trust in a *God-centered faith* through the aid of Mother Mary.

The Beatles, in the sixties and seventies, became rich and famous for their music. They had their share of worldly problems that seemed to accompany their chosen life styles. Through their gifts, they received the power of extraordinary musical accomplishment. Late in their careers, John Lennon and Paul McCartney produced their most popular song, "Let It Be." The message and feeling of "Let It Be," in my opinion, deemphasized the need to change the world and emphasized changing self. As we still ourselves, we know solutions will surface. Our moments of darkness and troubles lighten as we seek the resemblance of God. What is that resemblance? It is for each of us to discern.

It is most fascinating to hear the Beatles sing:

> When I find myself in times of trouble
> Mother Mary comes to me
> Speaking words of wisdom, Let it be.
> And in my hour of darkness
> She is standing right in front of me
> Speaking words of wisdom
> Let it be.

The Inner-Plane Experience

More ordinary people are having inner-plane experiences. Maybe it is because more people live on our planet. Maybe it is because we are in need of help, and possibly we are more open to such experiences. There is also the possibility we contracted for such support prior to entering this expression of Life.

There is no doubt that these experiences are pivotal and help the self realize the Self. Many persons are blessed to have these experiences. I feel blessed to share them with permission. They are part of the guidance system. How we interpret the guidance depends on the childlike awareness which rends the veil to the inner plane.

The Queen of Angels

The following is an example of an inner-plane experience which happened in 1978 to a young black female living in Atlanta, Georgia. Her name is Jacqueline M. Neal. Here is her "Inner-Plane Experience":

> While in my astral body and standing in my bedroom, I looked up and saw a beautiful female floating about four feet off the floor and about three feet in front of me. She wore a long, flowing dress. A white veil draped her hair and a brilliant golden halo lit her head and extended to her shoulders. Her presence and beauty so entranced me, I said joyfully, "I have seen an angel."
>
> As soon as I said that, her form changed. The halo disappeared and her veil turned blue. Even her features changed. Then I noticed she held at waist level a deeply weathered, wooden sign with one word carved into it: *Guadalupe.* I realized then she was a saint. As I looked at the sign, I heard her say: *Joanna, lill.*
>
> Then I saw her in a house, and it seemed as if she did not want others to know of her presence there. She sat sewing a beautiful design with an implement resembling a hook. She created flowers and designs with it on a pure, soft-looking white fabric. As I watched, she added loops of brown. Every stitch, design, and flower fitted together beautifully, creating a wedding garment of some kind but not a dress.

I'd venture to guess that in 1978 not many African American or white people in the southern part of the United States knew anything about Our Lady of Guada-

lupe. For centuries she has been the patron saint of all
Mexico. Once I gave an impromptu talk at an African
American Baptist church on the border of Mexico. Little did they know the story of Our Lady of Guadalupe
and little did they care until they received her message.
Not unlike Martin Luther King, Mary brought to a close
the inhumane treatment of people. Our Lady of Guadalupe used a simple, ordinary Indian named Juan Diego
to carry her message.

Now how did Jacqueline interpret her inner-plane experience? Is there some guidance for students of Truth
in Jacqueline's interpretation of this extraordinary event?
I feel there is. Here are her comments:

Jacqueline's Retrospective Comments

The beautiful woman, I realized upon awakening, was
Mary. She'd shown herself to me in her Christ form, the
beauty of which gave me the impression I'd seen an angel. It seems that she wanted to correct my mispercep-
tion and did so by changing her appearance and clothing.
Then she held up a sign to make sure I'd know her, but
in my soul-subconscious state I only knew her as a saint.

Her message came in two forms. The first is the message inherent in the word *Guadalupe*. I read about Mary's
appearances to Juan Diego and the impression of her image on his tilma. I believe Mary not only identified herself by using the sign *Guadalupe*, she was telling me the
message she gave Juan Diego also belonged to me, for
she is my mother also, spiritually speaking. She is a spiritual master and teacher of any who desire her guidance

and direction. Mary has played this role with me and has taught me to be humble, receptive and to experience her mercy.

Joanna, lill, Mary's words to me, consist of a related message. Joanna, as given in *the Metaphysical Bible Dictionary*,* symbolizes discernment and intuition in the soul aspect. It also perceives the truth about God's ability to provide whatever is needed . . . strength, purity, love, etc.

Lill is an obsolete form of *loll* and means "to throw one's self down." To me this means to humble oneself, to allow the personality and soul to experience spiritual humility, so that the Christ Self can take precedence in one's consicousness. This is an act of conscious desire and personal will: a choice. To express the compassion, mercy, and grace Mary demonstrates, we become humble and pure in heart in our soul and personality aspects.

This belief linked with meaning of the name Joanna indicates that as we humble ourselves, we will know the truth of God through spiritual discernment and intuition, for these qualities increase as we rely less upon our own mental machinations and more upon the cosmic knowledge and spiritual guidance of our Christ Self.

The wedding garment Mary sewed can symbolize preparation for the wedding of the soul (its natural body) with our personality self. As the soul and personality agree to turn within for guidance, discernment and intuitive knowing, as both become humbled and experience cleansing and clarity, a spiritual marriage occurs. Once these two aspects marry, they work in partnership, each dedicated to their unique role and function.

Once this relationship is steady, secure and trustworthy, this partnership is ready to be married (unify with)

*Published by Unity School of Christianity—*Ed.*

the Christ. When this mystical marriage occurs, we begin to experience our more multidimensional being. We gradually begin to express more consciously and purposefully Christ will and clarity, to direct God energy with purity of intent, to feel and to treat others with divine love, mercy, and grace . . . all as a natural expression of our soul and personality united with our Christ Self. And Mary (Christ-like Mary) is our teacher and way-shower; helping us to cleanse and purify our personality and soul to mirror the divine prototype.

Joseph Campbell

Jacqueline's discovery about the fusing together of soul and personality is important to students of Truth. This similar idea occurred to the celebrated teacher Joseph Campbell. Campbell's eclectic understanding of world cultures and religions is brilliant. His simple story-telling with vivid illustration made him a teacher of teachers. Bill Moyers, the renowned TV journalist, conducted an acclaimed PBS series called "The Power of Myth." In this series Campbell said, *I always tell my students to follow their bliss.* Bliss is another way to describe Divine Guidance. *Bliss is where the deep sense of being is from, and where your body and soul want to go. When you have that feeling, stay with it, and don't let anyone throw you off. I say don't be afraid to follow your bliss and doors will open where you didn't know they were going to be.* Campbell knew the fusing together of the soul and body is driven by our true aspirations of being in the world for God—God who is beyond description, resident in us as us. Joseph Campbell is correct.

My office door just opened further. The mail carriers brought this timely personal message from a man of science that understands the value of Divine Guidance: *As you grow in sensitivity to the vast universe within, you will discover the bliss that is your very nature. As you grow in awareness, your healing inner intelligence will flow to exactly where you need it,* writes Deepak Chopra, M.D.

PART VI

One Essential Nature: Within

IF WE LOOK deep enough into inner or outer space we discover that one essential nature is differentiating Itself everywhere. How can that be? Would God Itself destroy Itself through war, famine, disease or catastrophe? Certainly not if we understand God to be a Beneficent Presence. Yet we can observe a dark side of the Force, or rather a misuse of the Force. For instance, the people that choose to work in abortion clinics see a value in terminating fetuses to protect the mothers' health or civil rights. A person will ignore the civil law and kill the employees of the abortion clinic on the contradictory reasoning that they wish to preserve life. Indeed, all life is to be cherished. The ultimate irony is: the spiritual being never dies, the physical body is here for our learning.

Most wars are waged over struggles for power regarding religious, political or economical ideology. The mental sea of collected, unenlightened thought forms coming from us are never lost. These unenlightened thought forms that we call the dark side gravitate to misguided leaders like Hitler. Hitler thought he must preserve the purity of the Aryan race at the cost of human lives.

Just as the unenlightened thought forms gather and become a force field, the enlightened thought forms gather and support our intentions to preserve life. A leader emerges that becomes a beneficial presence. Joan of Arc, a peasant girl, is inner-directed by her essential divinity to become a general in the French army. Even though she led many soldiers into various battles, she never injured anyone. Although injured herself, she kept the momentum of battle going that put an end to a 100-year war. The collected beneficial thoughts, meditations and prayers found a volunteer leader in an intuitive, courageous, farm-girl.

Hitler cherished worldly, secular values of domination and superiority. Joan of Arc cherished her inner calling. She recognized that the essential nature of all beings is spiritual. The greater our attunement with our essential divinity, the more beneficially useful we are. Do we have a devotional faith in our race or do we have a faith in Spirit that animates all races and beings everywhere?

Ready to See

What does it take to look beyond appearances of life-threatening events? Do we have an unshakeable faith in Spirit, whom we know and absolutely trust here to teach us and guide us into remembrance of Itself? What are we to remember? What does it take for us to see? Are we ready to see the hidden, elucidating messages in our life-threatening events?

For me the hidden messages come fast, and sometimes

the answers are delayed. What works for me is persistent seeking, daily prayer and meditation. Sometimes it is important to know that we don't know. Spirit is the source of all knowing. Where is Spirit? *Pure Spirit is at the center of all form. Of Itself, It is formless but It is ever giving birth to form. The forms come and go but* It *goes on forever. We are some part of It,* says Ernest Holmes in *The Science of Mind.* The form is here for our learning. The Spirit knows what we need to learn. Here is an example of what I mean:

Ten years ago I detected a black mole about the size of a dime on my abdomen. My suspicions were confirmed by a dermatologist who biopsied the mole and told me it was malignant, a form of quick-spreading cancer. The dermatologist strongly urged me to see a plastic surgeon. She wanted a larger section removed to play it safe. I asked her if the lab report showed the border of the incision free of cancer. She said, "yes."

I asked myself the question, "What does it mean to be dying at the abdomen?" The immediate answer received came as a mentally invisible thought with what I needed to know. The abdominal surgery was performed in the *solar* plexus. The yellow rays of the sun are associated with this area. That is why we say a person scared is yellow, has no guts.

I had been too afraid to step out of my comfort zone and to express a ministry as a spiritual teacher. The message I received was *I am dying to express as a spiritual teacher but failing to go where Spirit would take me.* I took the message to heart. I decided further surgery was unnecessary and became a minister in a small desert community.

A Few Years Later

A few years later an event happened that seemed un-
related to the message I had received earlier. This event
seemed weird, hard to believe and more difficult to understand. I share it to show that over a prolonged period
my point of view and attitude shifted with the gathering
of new information. I share with you my shifting understanding of reality. I pray that some of these shared experiences may be meaningful to other students of Truth.

One evening around midnight I awoke suddenly from
a sound half-hour of sleep. I felt a powerful presence of
energy come through my closed bedroom door. The presence seemed to move toward my sleeping wife. I instinctively opposed it. As I did this mentally, it turned toward
me. I could see nothing. I felt as if a huge, industrial
vacuum cleaner was sucking me out of my bed, feet first.
Out of desperation I spoke the name Jesus and Mary.
Suddenly the intrusive power left. I assure you this was
not a dream. After some deliberation, I allowed my wife
to sleep through this ordeal. I placed an icon of Jesus and
Mary from my office at the head of our bed. I fell asleep
an hour later in prayer.

In the morning as my wife Bobbe awoke, I shared this
experience with her. She felt goosebumps as I told her
the story. She tried to speak and discovered she had
laryngitis.

What was this intrusive, invisible presence? Was this
the dark side of the force? Was this an evil discarnate
spirit with strange use of power? Perhaps! Did this have
to do with my willingness to venture into other invisible

realms in my healing prayer work? What woke me out
of a very sound sleep to come to Bobbe's defense? These
are questions I had eight years ago. And now some new
information merged with some older information to produce some startling discoveries.

Little Did I Know

A surprise turn of events reawakened an unexpected oc-
currence. Twenty-eight years ago, my friend Jack and I
witnessed a light-source similar to the one used in the *Star
Trek* series for beaming people up or down. This was not
a weather balloon, a misguided missile or another excuse
to explain or cover up a UFO sighting. It was simply a
round cylinder, a vertical shaft of light, maybe five feet
in diameter. The shaft was almost 200 yards long and fell
close to earth. Jack and I observed the light from about
a mile away. We watched it intently for two to three
minutes before it vanished.

Over recent years I had become aware of alleged UFO
activity and abductions by alien beings. Dr. John Mack,
a Harvard psychiatrist, and others have discovered that
through hypnosis, patients can recall things about abductions we might not otherwise know. They have noted in
the many cases where UFO abductees suffer memory loss
that the block is removed under hypnosis. It is important
for psychiatrist and psychotherapist not to make sugges-
tions that would color or influence the outcome of their
patients' spontaneous response to treatment.

Eight months ago, I asked Dr. Jean Clements, a psychotherapist and long-time friend, to guide me through some light hypnosis. My intention was to see if I could recall anything from that intrusive event years ago. Here is my new discovery, believe it or not.

Believe It or Not

To be an explorer in inner or outer space, it helps to be a little crazy. Perhaps it is more crazy to hold on to beliefs that limit our receptivity to grow. Here is what I received eight months ago under supervised hypnosis.

For the hypnosis to work for me, I needed to get my intellectual considerations out of the way. I entered my feeling nature and felt cramps in my lower leg that brought pictures to mind. I verbalized what I saw. Someone took me out of my bedroom through two closed doors that exited to the rear of our house. I was drawn through a beam into a space vehicle. My abductors had slight builds and large, bald, gray heads shaped somewhat like a light bulb. I was placed on a clean, modern-looking, high surgical table with my feet elevated into some metal stirrups. The surgeon stood to my left at the middle of the table. He worked in my abdomen. I sensed he, she or it cleaned residue or growth from my previous cancer operation. I was returned to my bedroom.

Dr. Clements and I finished the session with discussion. I told her of the frightening experience I attributed earlier to an unknown, invasive force, a force which now seemed to be a beneficial presence. I was helped mysteriously. The surgery caused no pain or bleeding.

Did I image and feel all this? Yes. Was the experience a remembrance of what actually happened? Probably. Can I say for sure? No. I had not intended to share these extraordinary events until I was reminded of something during my morning meditation. For about five or six years, I experienced severe leg cramps while lying in bed. To get relief, I had to get up and vigorously massage my calves, the usual area of cramps. Thank God, I only had one cramp, in one leg, at one time.

The new insight is this: the cramps were most prevalent after my alleged abduction. They persisted until my hypnosis session with Dr. Clements approximately a year ago. For the past year I have had no leg cramps. Could my feeling nature have remembered and stored the unexpressed pain of my legs held high in stirrups for a prolonged period?

Each new insight takes us to new frontiers of self knowing Self. Thank God. Each new revelation shows us a Beneficial Presence at work. At the center of all things Spirit is giving birth to change. Change is brought through the Divine Mama, prompted by the Divine Papa. Let us look more deeply into the Divine Mother and Divine Father principles.

Humility

What does it mean to be humble or meek? It means to be devoid of arrogance, haughtiness, pretentiousness, snobbishness, conceit, superiority, vanity, vainglory, pomposity, disdain, boastfulness, presumptuousness, contemptuousness, and glamour. These attributes give us spiritual Alzheimer's disease. We don't remember our essential divinity. *But the meek shall inherit the earth; and shall delight themselves in the abundance of peace* (Psalms 37:11). David, who wrote this psalm, knew that the principle of peace is an essential nature of divinity. To be at ease is to be revealing our essential divinity through the portal of spiritual awareness. The key that transcends these troublesome thought forms of self-importance is true humility.

The famous Sermon on the Mount repeats what David sang in his psalm on meekness. The Sermon on the Mount suggests ways of being in the world that transcend the vanities of a personhood or separate self. Matthew, who recorded the sermon, changed his name from Levi to rid himself of the stigma that went with his former tax-collecting profession. Like other reporters and disciples, Matthew was not interested in the personhood of Jesus of Nazareth. Matthew was interested in his teachings and his deeds. The Sermon on the Mount starts with *Blessed are the poor in spirit: for theirs is the kingdom of heaven* (Matthew 5:3).

Poor in spirit means to be emptied or devoid of the thoughts, feelings or activities that give us a false sense of separation from our essential divinity. The proactive choice is to aspire to true humility, which opens the portals to inspired living. We do inherit the earth by expressing the will-to-good as found in our essential nature. The Kingdom of Heaven is brought to earth through us as we live the Principle and practice the Presence.

"The Weak Finish Last"

"The weak finish last" is often confused with being humble or meek. Being weak is often associated with our being humble, saying we are sorry or admitting we are wrong. The truth is, when we are fearful we want to cover up, find fault and place blame. The power-seeking, controlling, manipulative, competitive, anger-driven personalities are often considered strong by worldly standards and yet really miss the mark by spiritual standards. True humility opens our awareness to what God wants. As we learn to live the principle, we express a deeper appreciation for the allness of Spirit.

Often the spiritual path (any path) is sprinkled with pain and suffering, and the disciples of Truth endure much. It is equally true that the spiritual path is suffused with expanded awareness, intuitive knowing, blessed assurance and Divine Guidance. Why? Because we take the time to be silent, contemplative and expectant. Our ground of being is spiritual. We learn to think with our hearts and express life in harmony with our Source. Our Source is absolute Love, and in Love we find our identity in One Life, One Mind, One Power. There is no other. Our sense of personhood is no longer viewed as a separate self. We are like an individual cell in the body of God. Christ, Buddha, Immaculate Mother and others emerged as primordial archetypes that have lost their sense of separation and have come home to absolute, pervasive Being. The Archetype or divine prototype exists in all of us. True humility helps us lose our false, imagined sense of personal power (personhood) and regain our true identity.

In each courageous act we lose a sense of being here for oneself, or for others, and we fulfill our greater purpose. The truly courageous individuals are motivated by unconditional love, which is of God. The "unmeek" person is motivated by fear and lives in the shadow of true love. Fear stirs within us a restlessness that only true love can satisfy. Love is filled with gratitude, and it is with gratitude that I share this next story, which is worth more than the price of this book. It is a priceless story that reveals the synchronicity of divine Guidance working through us.

Synchronicity

This latest development stimulates my mind and I can hardly wait to share it because it demonstrates that Divine Guidance is always with us in the ordinary and extraordinary aspects of our lives. Here is the background:

Forty-seven years ago I enjoyed being an uncle to my 3-year-old nephew Kenny. I would ride him on the handlebars of my bike. We had great fun together. He was my brother René's first child. Due to a freak mishap, my nephew died and his younger brother nearly died from the same disease, smallpox. An older cousin who had just had a smallpox vaccination had rubbed up against the two boys' open wounds caused by the skin disorder eczema. Needless to say, the family was devastated by the loss of Kenny. No one realized how hard my brother took the death of his first son. René disappeared. At the time of the tragedy and René's subsequent disappearance I was fourteen and my brother almost twenty-one.

Some forty-seven years later, René experienced the sudden death of his twenty-three-year-old stepson, Kenny. Kenny and a male companion were unexpectedly shot and killed. His murder devastated the family. René was very close to Kenny and the other children that he had raised in this marriage. René had a total of eight children in several marriages. What are the odds that he would have two sons die before him, both named Kenny?

Just this week, my brother shared what had happened upon the death of his first son. René ran away from Boston, where we then lived, to Florida. He told me, ''I was so angry when Aunt Katherine told me, 'God must have wanted Kenny; that is why He took him.' I was infuriated. Against all family advice, I ran away for a week. When I arrived in Florida, I did not have any money. I went to a hotel where I obtained a part-time job in the boiler room. The maintenance supervisor was a good man. He gave me a place to sleep and money for food. I made up my mind then and there, if death can suddenly rob you of life, *I'm going to live the time remaining to the fullest.*''

As a distant observer of a considerably older brother, it is safe to say from the stories he confided to me that René was a man of the world. I say *was* because, after the death of his stepson, my brother's life was transformed by an awesome event. His values, his beliefs, shifted to a deeper spiritual awareness. "Beyond all comprehension it was the most beautiful and glorious experience in my life when my stepson, Kenny, appeared to me as an angel," said René.

It is difficult for anyone to describe accurately an encounter with the Other Side. My brother calls this 15 to 20 minute experience he had with Kenny #2, "Heaven." René's experience was similar to what other people have experienced in what is termed *near-death*. You will read later that my brother's profound experience was not prompted by his near-death; his experience rose out of sincere gratitude expressed to God. Through God's grace his orientation to life changed from being here in the now for oneself and/or for one's family, to being here *in the eternal Present*. His understanding went from worldly values to profound spiritual awareness. What I hope to make clear is the synchronicity and subtle nature of Divine Guidance. I am still in awe of what we discovered in the next step with Spirit.

René said, "I sure have been pondering why God took my two sons with the same name, Kenny." I said to René, "I am going to look up the name Kenny. I feel we may find a clue in the name." I was amazed at what I found as a definition in my *Webster's New Collegiate Dictionary*:

> **ken** 1. (a) the range of vision; (b) sight, view . . . "'tis double death to drown in ken of shore"—Shak.
> 2. the range of perception, understanding, or knowledge

Double death of two sons named Kenny gave René the full range of perception—a perception that goes from living for oneself to being a beneficial presence for God. It is important to note that no matter how far René strayed, he regularly prayed or conversed privately with God.

Now permit me to go back in time approximately fourteen months before that so you can get a ''feel'' for the synchronicity in our guidance system.

The Call

Eleven o'clock one evening the phone rang. I got out of bed to answer it, wondering who would intrude on my privacy at this late hour.

A strange young lady's voice said, ''I am Kenny's fiancee. He is in jail and asked me to call you for help, Uncle Charlie.'' I remembered my brother, René, had a stepson whose name was Kenny. I had met this twenty-three-year-old nephew only once or twice and would not be able to pick him out in a crowd.

I asked the young lady if she had called my brother or his wife, Alice, who were living apart. She had tried them first without any luck. ''I don't know why Kenny wanted you to call me, I don't think he needs a minister—he needs a lawyer or bail bondsman,'' I said, dismissing her. I thought no more about it until three months later.

Three Months Later

I was in Virginia Beach at an A.R.E. (Association of Research and Enlightenment) Easter conference doing a book-signing of my latest work. While at the conference, I received word from my relatives in Washington that my nephew Kenny and his friend were shot and killed in Huntington Beach, California by an unknown assailant. I shared this information with my wife, Bobbe. She reminded me of Kenny's attempt to reach me through his fiancee three months before.

"Aha!" I knew in a flash that somewhere in his subconscious mind Kenny must have known he would need assistance from a minister. Coincidentally, I had just learned an effective way of helping individuals in other dimensions of life. In my meditation I had learned to help people on the Other Side. I got a strong feeling that Kenny needed help. I was led to help him. I found him in a state of confusion, in a place of darkness. Not an unusual experience for those whose lives are abruptly uprooted from this expression of life. Taking Kenny by the hand, I led him into the light and bid him farewell on his next assignment.

As a child, I was taught to pray for the faithfully departed. As an adult approaching sixty, I feel it is not for me to judge who departed faithfully. I do understand the great value in properly directed prayer. I am still learning the value of directing the vital forces (etheric vitality) in a beneficial manner, according to His will.

Synchronicity is everywhere operating behind the

scenes. Sometimes I feel privileged to understand the beneficent working of Divine Guidance behind the scenes.

The Next Scene

Three weeks ago I was viewing a television program I had never seen before called *From the Other Side*. Carol, whom you may remember as the mother who requested help for her possessed son, James, in Part III, suggested I watch the program. She was being interviewed on the show.

After viewing the program, I left the television on while cleaning up my breakfast dishes. I heard a familiar voice come from the TV. It was Alice, my brother's wife. She was looking for help to find the murderer of their son, Kenny. Alice seemed relentlessly compelled to discover the reason for this brutal crime.

I called René at work and Alice answered the phone. She informed me that the TV program was a re-run and she was still using any resources to locate her son's killer. I asked her, "Did René tell you about how I was able to assist Kenny soon after his transition to the Other Side?" Her reply was "No," and I repeated the story to her. Alice said, "You must talk to René; he had a most interesting and extraordinary experience."

Immediately I called my brother, who answered the phone with a new vitality in his voice. This was a transformed person from the one I shared earlier in this book (in the Prelude; again as carpet salesman in a humorous

story; and as a gambler who used his extraordinary winnings to finance a trip to visit our terminally ill mother).
Now I have the thrill of sharing his experience of the
Other Side.

The Other Side

Here is what René related to me:

> Charlie, I always believed in God and was very private
> about it. Just about every day I thank God for good
> health and for loved ones. Sometimes, while driving my
> carpet van, I would look up at the sky and talk with God,
> particularly when I was confused. You know, I have not
> led a model life and I can't explain some of the things I
> have done. Perhaps I would have been happier with one
> wife and a house full of kids. It just did not work out that
> way. I wish to God it had. I was never too sure about life
> hereafter until my recent visitation from Kenny.

I said, "Tell me about this visitation from your son!"

> It was about six o'clock one morning. I was sitting at
> my desk in my family room looking through the sliding
> glass door as the sun came up. I commented to myself
> "What a beautiful day!" I walked outside on my patio
> past the chain link beyond the pool area. I murmured to
> myself, "Thank you, God, for this beautiful day."
> All of a sudden this radiant being appeared, like an
> angel. It was Kenny. My body was filled with so much
> energy that my hair stood up on end all over my body.

You know, like having the hair on the back of your neck stand up when you get scared.

"Were you scared?" I asked.

No; there was like an electrical current that surrounded and protected me. It was the most beautiful day of my life. I really thought God was calling me. I never dreamed that He would send my son to me as a whole person to converse with me as an angel. Beyond all my comprehension, it was the most beautiful and glorious experience in my life.

"Please tell me more, René. What happened?"

For the next fifteen to twenty minutes by the pool, I did not exist as a person on earth, whole and alive. God gave me a sample of what Heaven is like, and it is beyond all comprehension as we know it and study it on earth.

All my life I was troubled about the death of my three-year-old son, Kenny. I never understood why he had to die; and now I do. I was shown my first son, Kenny, and all the people I ever knew who had died.

"What about our Mom, is she all right?" I asked.

Mom, Dad and everyone are wonderful and in a place beyond my ability to describe. This miracle has made it possible for me to know that life goes on forever. When my job is done on Earth, I know I will be with Jesus for all eternity, sharing love with everyone.

"What did your angelic son, Kenny, have to say?"

He asked me to help Alice, who was taking his death too hard. Alice is visiting Kenny's grave site daily. I agreed to help her.

Two weeks went by. I was frightened to tell anyone of this strange, unbelievable meeting with my son. Kenny appeared a second time. He encouraged me again to help Alice. "She really needs your help," he said.

Charlie, I needed the second appearance to overcome my fear. I was not sure if I was going crazy. You know me; things have to be proven to me so I can understand. Now that I am helping Alice, I have other visits with Kenny, at my request. And another strange thing about this is, Alice had given me this book to read after Kenny's death. It is called *Embraced by the Light*, by Betty J. Eadie. Since my heavenly visit I cannot put it down. I have read it many times. I had not even noticed the wonderful inscription by Alice which reads:

Rene,

Thank you for giving me strength and always being here for me. May this book bring you some of the peace you have given to me.

Loving you and thanks,
Alice

Rene and I talked for almost two hours. He no longer sells carpets in the old way. He goes into a home first as a compassionate being ready to serve the greater "Good." Through amazing grace, he has been activated to a higher level of service. Rene absolutely knows he is not responsible for the change that is taking place within him. What he does know is that he has the ability to respond with love and compassion to any circumstance.

"Charlie, this may be hard to believe. Three months ago I would have killed the murderer of my son without any hesitation. I have truly forgiven the murderer. I feel no malice for anyone."

For the first time in almost sixty years, René said to me, "I love you." I really felt his sincerity. René was able to surrender his indifference and I was able to give up my self-righteousness to treasure this wonderful gift of love. It was worth waiting all these years to meet my brother in the Spirit.

Yes, it is Spirit that is guiding each of us to discern our purpose for being here. Divine Guidance is everywhere present and more obvious as we become more interested in It.

By the way, if you remember in the Prelude of this book, I wrote about having invited my brother several times to attend a self-awareness training. It was the training that helped me come to the realization that I really loved him twenty years ago. René informed me that he went to a Guest Seminar, like the one I had invited him to twenty years ago, at the invitation of his son Michael.

René said, "I stood up and talked for forty-five minutes and it was not me talking." (I did not ask him, but I knew it was the Holy Spirit, the Presence of God that uses us according to Its will, as we are able to get our sense of a separate self out of the way.) "The crowd was spellbound listening to the words coming out of my mouth. I don't even know what I said. I signed up for the training and I know I am going there to help others," René told me.

René, thank you for sharing this intimate story. Most of us can appreciate the glamour, the attraction of pursuing worldy values and the importance of turning within to spiritual values.

Glamour

The glamour of false security can distract us from our innate purpose for being here. My colleague and friend Reverend Margarita operates a healing center for a poor neighborhood in Mexico. She relates an example of glamour, of false security.

Margarita was generously offered a free home to live in beside her daughter in an affluent neighborhood in California. It was a glamorous place and offered many perks that were missing in Mexico, such as inside flush toilets, paved streets. Margarita stayed in Mexico and has helped thousands of people get well at her free-of-cost healing center.

Glamour is often a trap that sidetracks us from our main purpose for being here. We become enchanted, spellbound or false-security-driven. For example, a teacher wrestling with the glamour of self-importance took all sincere compliments with genuine gratitude. He would express his thanks for the compliment while silently giving thanks to God. Why thanks to God? Because he felt taking personal credit would give him a sense of self-importance, a swelled head. Giving credit where credit is due, we give the Source of all talents the credit for our talents. Again, it requires humility.

True self-esteem is not infatuation with self. Self-esteem comes through the realization that we are being here for God in fulfilling our part in the plan. As we become more humble, God as infinite Love and boundless Intelligence is more evident in the plan. The plan within the Divine Guidance system is to awaken us to be all we truly are. If we truly are children of God it behooves us to seek Its resemblance. Infatuation with our own intellect, our own knowlege, distracts us from our Divine Guidance. Our life is like a tree; we must respect our ground of being. Our ground of being is rooted in Spirit. Without Spirit we are nothing.

Tree of Life

Eating the forbidden fruit from the tree of self-knowledge was the downfall of Adam and Eve. The Fall created a sense of separation from God. An identity crisis occurred; the form or phenomenal presentation of Spirit was viewed by spirit as separate from itself. This way of thinking perpetuated a mental sea of feelings and thought forms not representative of Truth. Thought forms and feelings that are less than spiritually true give us an experience of unreality, such as death, illness, disease, etc. We have made the temporal (phenomenal presentation) or worldy values more important than the true qualities resident in Spirit.

The tree of life is resident in Spirit. The tree of life is a metaphor for the resemblance of Self as a divine prototype. *The mind, "cleansed" of attachments to merely secular aims, desires, and fears, is released to spiritual rapture,* says Joseph Campbell. As we aspire to express the will-to-good, spiritual rapture is ignited within us. Our aspiration meets our inspiration, our practicing the Principle brings to our awareness the Presence. The eternal Father is well pleased with the immortal Son and blessed in spiritual rapture by the divine Mother. At this holy instant we are remembering that our roots lie within the divine prototype. The tree of Life as a symbol is a reminder to value the diversity in the spirit of unity.

Some of us are inner-directed or motivated to seek the resemblance of God. Our hope is to change our way of being in the world, by honoring all life, surrendering our false knowledge of a separate self, and identifying with our ididual, divine prototype in following our bliss. Shedding light is the joy of the soul. Light subdues restlessness and makes for beneficial activity.

Gratitude

I would like to thank all the wonderful contributors to this book. God is so good in bringing us together. Life is so precious. I salute and honor the Life in you. God blesses you. And should we meet near the garden of Eden with our clothes off, you can identify me by a scar on my rear. I didn't want to leave the garden. God had to kick me good to move me out to my next assignment. I was reluctant to go.

On my previous venture I witnessed a serious accident. My pet dogma was run over by my karma on a temporal highway, in the state of anxiety. As the driver of the vehicle which caused the mishap, I got so distraught I thought my no-fault insurance had expired. I wanted to blame someone or something for this painful incident. I desperately needed help to rid myself of making things too serious. I prayed for guidance. An inner voice suggested an operation on my psyche calling for a funny-bone transplant. Fortuitously, I found a funny-bone donor. The transplant operation went well, but I am still concerned! I still feel guilty! It is my fault that there is someone without a funny-bone! Some eternal being running around without humor.

Let that [humor] therefore abide in you, which ye have heard from the beginning. If that which you have heard from the beginning shall remain in you, ye also shall continue in the Son, and in the Father. And this is the promise that he hath promised us, even eternal life (I John 2:24,25). I hope St. John does not complain to the Boss that I added *humor* to his holy words.

In the next section, Part VII, of this book I share with you some of the prayers that help stimulate and support our intuitive growth.

PART VII

PRAYERS EFFECTIVE AND AFFECTIVE

Effective and Affective

EFFECTIVE PRAYER has a positive intent with a specific purpose, spoken or contemplated with faith, affirming a desired result as though it has already occurred. For example, speak with conviction or meditate on these words knowing they are so: *I seek to Love, not hate*, or *I am loving and I do not hate*. The desired effect is established in the present tense and creates an effective prayer.

Please notice, this prayer uses positive and negative words with positive intent. The key idea is *with positive intent*. Remember, words are more than thought forms, they are power-filled elementals or holodynes that leave a lasting impression in the holodynamic memory bank. We must be careful of what we pray for, for ourselves, for others. The desired effect is established in mind *now*. There is no postponement. The answer is in the prayer. We always pray for the highest and best ''good'' of those concerned.

Affective Prayer is an effective prayer expressed with feeling. Use both effective and affective prayer, and feel the power within the prayer.

Here is a wonderful prayer from a beneficial presence known as the Tibetan; it is called the "Unification Mantra." This prayer is found in the book *The Externalization of the Hierarchy*, which was dictated to Alice A. Bailey by The Tibetan. The hierarchy is made up of individuals that found their way home.

Unification Mantra

The children of God are one and I am one with them.

I seek to love, not hate;

I seek to serve and not exact due service;

I seek to heal, not hurt.

Let pain bring due reward of light and love.

Let the soul control the outer form,

And life, and all events,

And bring to light the love

That underlies the happening of the times.

Let vision come and insight,

Let the future stand revealed,

Let inner union demonstrate and outer

Separation be gone.

Let love prevail,

Let all love.

I suggest the above mantra be recited every day by the students of Truth. Why? Because *It is a modernized and mystically worded version of the one used widely in Atlantean days during the period of the ancient conflicts of which the present is an effect. For many of you this mantra will be in the nature of a recovery of an old and well-known form of words,* wrote Alice A. Bailey.

Hide-and-Seek

God provides ascended teachers who have mastered the principles of spiritual Life and live in the Presence. Some of these saints and sages are the Heavenly Hosts, the helpers. Their resemblance to God is immaculate. They are not to be worshiped. Jesus did not ask to be worshiped. For many, Jesus is the perfect incarnation of Spirit. He abides in the Spirit. That same Spirit is resident in all. Jesus gave all the credit to the Father within. This is our best clue. We find Spirit in the silence and quiet of our own minds. Worldly glamour, excitement and power distract us from direct intuitive knowing.

Effective and affective daily praying aids us in filling each precious moment with an inner sense of Joy, Love and Peace that goes beyond the limitations of temporal awareness. Seek God's guidance. Live it. Be it.

Seek and you shall find. It helps to understand and to know that what we are seeking is also seeking us. In living spiritual principles we must be aware of the trap of self-righteousness. Our "holier-than-thou" attitude is confirming a sense of separation, an unforgiving way of being in the world. It is equally a trap to think that we are worthless and unworthy. God knows our true worth. Let us know, love and serve the will-to-good as we develop right human relations and foster undistorted reverence and humility. In doing so we are more amenable to Divine Guidance.

Our spiritual aspirations open the "eye of the needle," the portal to the center of inspiration. Inspiration guides us to express what God already knows of Its absolute, beneficial nature. God is Love. No one who expresses genuine love needs guidance. Most of us fall short or miss the mark and can use the extraordinary, diverse and pervasive assistance of an unlimited, extraordinary guidance system.

God provides many wonderful role-models and guides. They are Beneficial Presences living as Christlike expressions. Such is The Tibetan, who gave us the aforementioned mantra. Such is the mother of Jesus who is known by many names. So is the Buddha, and so on.

Spiritual discernment is a tool we can develop as we practice the Principles and live in the Presence. As the will and the intellect are married in a holy union with love, we deeply sense God working through us in extraordinary ways. *When both the intellect and will are quiet and passive to the expression of the eternal Word and Spirit, and when thy soul is winged up above that which is temporal . . . then the eternal Hearing, Seeing, and Speaking will be revealed in thee,* per Jakob Boehme.

Benediction

Here is a closing prayer of Benediction by the omnipresent Holy Comforter. God can use anyone as a comforter. We also understand that God provides direct
revelation of Truth and that the Holy Comforter is resident in all life. Here is a prayer designed to invoke help
and to open ourselves to more Divine Guidance.

Raise your arms like a V. Imagine a ball of light like
the sun about fourteen inches above your head. Repeat
these words:

May the Holy Comforter show us the light we seek,

Give us the strong aid of compassion and wisdom.

There is a peace that passes understanding;

It abides in the hearts of those who live in the eternal.

There is a power that makes all things new;

It lives and moves in those who know the self as One.

May that peace brood over us, that power uplift us,

Till we understand that we are here for God,

And God is here for us, always guiding and providing.

Prayer Affirming Guidance

There is one Life, one Spirit, one Mind expressing Itself every-where. It is expressing Its Self through me, as me. Each impulse, each breath, each heart-beat brings me into greater appreciation of Spirit's activity. I am an activity of Spirit. I am living fully in accordance with Divine Guidance. Giving thanks to thee, O God, I release any sense of separation. I joyfully have found my true resemblance in Thee. Amen.

Bibliography

Bailey, Alice A., *The Externalizations of the Hierarchy* (New York: Lucis Publishing Co., 1957).

————. *Initiation, Human and Solar* (New York: Lucis Publishing Co., 1970).

Bracey, Hyler; Rosenblum, Jack; Sanford, Aubrey; Trueblood, Roy, *Managing from the Heart* (New York: Delacorte Press, Bantam Doubleday Dell Publishing Group, 1990).

Brinkley, Dannion (with Paul Perry), *Saved by the Light* (New York: Villard Books, 1994).

Bucke, Richard Maurice, M.D., *Cosmic Consciousness* (New York: E. P. Dutton and Co., 1901).

Butterworth, Eric, *In the Flow of Life* (New York: Harper & Row, 1957).

Campbell, Joseph, *The Power of Myth, with Bill Moyers* (New York: Mystic Fire Video, 1988).

Cayce, Edgar, *A Search for God*, Books I and II (Virginia Beach, Va.: Edgar Cayce Foundation, 1991).

Chellis, Marcia, *Ordinary Women, Extraordinary Lives* (New York: Penguin Books USA, 1992).

Eadie, Betty, *Embraced by the Light* (Placerville, Calif.: Gold Leafe Press, 1992).

Hittleman, Richard, *Guide to Yoga Meditation* (New York: Bantam Books, 1977).

Holmes, Ernest, *The Science of Mind* (New York: G. P. Putnam's Sons, 1938).

Hora, Thomas, *Existential Metapsychiatry* (Orange, Calif.: PAGL Press, 1983).

Lennon, John; McCartney, Paul, *Great Songs of Lennon & McCartney* (New York: Random House, 1974).

Markides, C. Kyriacos, *Fire in the Heart* (New York: Paragon House, 1990).

————. *The Magus of Stovolos* (London: Penguin Books, 1985).

Michael, Arnold, *Blessed Among Women* (Westlake Village, Calif.: Gray Publications, 1986).

Redfield, James, *The Celestine Prophecy* (Hoover, Ala.: Satori Publishing, 1994).

Scheeben, Mathias, *The Glories of Divine Grace* (1886).

Sinetar, Marsha, *Ordinary People As Monk and Mystic* (Mahwah, N.J.: Paulist Press, 1986).

Twain, Mark, *The Complete Essays of Mark Twain* (Garden City, N.Y.: Doubleday & Company, 1963).

Woods, Ralph L., *The World Treasury of Religious Quotations* (New York: Hawthorn Books, 1966).

Woolf, V. Vernon, *Holodynamics* (Tucson, Ariz.: Harbinger House, 1990).

Yatiswarananda, Swami, *The Divine Life* (Mylapore, Madras, India: Sri Ramakrishna Math)

Dictionary quotations are from *Merriam Webster's Collegiate Dictionary*.

Biblical quotations and references are from *The New Analytical Bible and Dictionary of the Bible*, the Authorized King James Version, the American Standard Version, and *The Holy Bible: From Ancient Eastern Texts*, by George M. Lamsa, trans.

Cool Restaurants
Tokyo

teNeues

Imprint

Editor:	Sabina Marreiros
Editorial coordinators:	Ellen Nepilly, Rie Okubo, Kumiko Nishimura, Yuko Miyazawa
Photos (location):	Courtesy Soho's (Le Dragon Bleu, Olives), Courtesy Maimon (Maimon), Eisuke (If), Soho Junichi (Bamboo Bar), Haruhiko Kitai (Bandol Wine Bar & Restaurant, Las Chicas), Nacasa & Partners (Daidaiya, Oto Oto), Martin Pes (Le Cocon), Okada (Bamboo Bar), Shibazaki (Tower's Restaurant Coucagno), Kozo Takayama (Bape Café!?). All other Photos by Roland Bauer and Martin Nicholas Kunz.
Introduction:	Masaaki Takahishi
Layout & Pre-press:	Thomas Hausberg
Imaging:	Jan Hausberg
Translations:	Hausner & Manz-Gulde GbR-OTC-International Nina Hausberg (English, German / Recipes)

Produced by fusion publishing GmbH
www.fusion-publishing.com

Published by teNeues Publishing Group

teNeues Publishing Company
16 West 22nd Street, New York, NY 10010, USA
Tel.: 001-212-627-9090, Fax: 001-212-627-9511

teNeues Book Division
Kaistraße 18, 40221 Düsseldorf, Germany
Tel.: 0049-(0)211-994597-0, Fax: 0049-(0)211-994597-40

teNeues Publishing UK Ltd.
P.O. Box 402, West Byfleet, KT14 7ZF, Great Britain
Tel.: 0044-1932-403509, Fax: 0044-1932-403514

teNeues France S.A.R.L.
4, rue de Valence, 75005 Paris, France
Tel.: 0033-1-55766205, Fax: 0033-1-55766419

www.teneues.com

ISBN:	ISBN 3-8238-4590-X

© 2004 teNeues Verlag GmbH + Co. KG, Kempen

Printed in Germany

Bibliographic information published by
Die Deutsche Bibliothek. Die Deutsche Bibliothek lists
this publication in the Deutsche Nationalbibliografie;
detailed bibliographic data is available in the Internet
at http://dnb.ddb.de.

Contents

Introduction

In the last two decades, the quality of Japan's restaurants, bars and cafes has improved beyond all recognition in terms of both food and the interiors.
The main thrust behind this transformation was the gourmet boom that hit Japan in the nineties, sparked by a sudden increase in the popularity of Italian food. Naturally, there were many establishments offering fine international dining in Tokyo before the boom, not to mention the existence of superior Japanese restaurants of long standing, but these were too few to meet the demand of the general public. Now, however, it has become possible to consume the kind of sophisticated ingredients and dishes that could previously only be appreciated at high class Japanese-style restaurants. For a reasonable price you can easily find not only non-Japanised international fare, but also a variety of fusion cuisine, for example Bape Cafe!?, creative Japanese dishes that have become popular particularly among the younger crowd.
Tokyo has become a dining capital on a par with New York, a development also reflected in the increasingly stylish interiors of eating establishments. The city is seeing a diversification and fusion of different styles, giving birth to a new style all of its own. Typical Japanese design is being reinterpreted from a Western European perspective, allowing designers to create spin-offs of a variety of Japanese styles. You see a lot of good examples of such new style in Oto Oto, Daidaiya, Cube Zen, Naka Naka, Zipang etc.
Japanese designers, as well as those from abroad, are finding stimulation in the Nouvel Japonism overflowing in Tokyo to take design in new directions. They are discovering new styles and creating new design vocabulary as you see in this book.
By inviting attention to the refinement of the dining environment, these beautiful interiors can only add to the gastronomic experience, creating a vibrant artistic marriage that can be seen throughout Tokyo.

Masaaki Takahishi

5

Einleitung

In den letzten zwei Jahrzehnten hat sich die Qualität der japanischen Restaurants, Bars und Cafés enorm verbessert, sowohl was die Küche als auch was die Innenarchitektur betrifft.

Der Hauptgrund für diesen Wandel ist der Gourmet-Boom, der Japan in den neunziger Jahren ereilte, ausgelöst von einem sprunghaften Anstieg der Popularität der italienischen Küche. Selbstverständlich gab es in Tokio schon vor diesem Boom zahlreiche gastronomische Betriebe, die feine internationale Küche anboten, ganz zu schweigen von den seit langem bestehenden hervorragenden japanischen Restaurants. Doch ihre Anzahl war zu gering, um der allgemeinen Nachfrage gerecht zu werden. Heute ist es jedoch möglich, die feinen Zutaten und Gerichte zu genießen, die früher nur in den erstklassigen Restaurants mit japanischer Küche verzehrt werden konnten. Zu einem angemessenen Preis lassen sich nicht nur Restaurants mit nichtjapanischer internationaler Küche finden, sondern auch eine Auswahl an sogenannten „Mischküchen", wie z. B. das Bape Café!?, das kreative japanische Gerichte anbietet, die vor allem bei einem jüngeren Publikum sehr beliebt sind.

Tokio hat sich zur einer Metropole des Essens entwickelt, die New York in nichts nachsteht. Diese Entwicklung spiegelt sich auch in den zunehmend stilvolleren Ausstattungen der Gastronomiebetriebe wieder. Die Stadt erlebt eine Veränderung und eine Verschmelzung der einzelnen Stile, wodurch ein ganz neuer eigener Stil entsteht. Typisch japanisches Design wird aus der westeuropäischen Perspektive neu interpretiert; und dies ermöglicht es Designern, Abwandlungen einer Vielzahl japanischer Stilarten zu schaffen. Oto Oto, Daidaiya, Cube Zen, Naka Naka oder Zipang sind gute Beispiele für diesen neuen Stil.

Japanische und ausländische Designer finden Inspiration im „Neo-Japonism"-Stil, der sich stark ausbreitet und das Design in Tokio in neue Richtungen lenkt. Sie entdecken neue Stilarten und schaffen ein neues Designvokabular, dem dieses Buch nachspürt.

Indem sie die Aufmerksamkeit auf die ansprechende Umgebung lenken, ergänzen diese schönen Interieurs das gastronomische Erlebnis und führen zu einer lebendigen künstlerischen Verbindung, die in ganz Tokio anzutreffen ist.

Masaaki Takahishi

6

Introduction

Au cours des vingt dernières années, la qualité des restaurants, bars et cafés japonais s'est tant améliorée au niveau des cartes mais aussi des intérieurs qu'ils en sont devenus méconnaissables.

Ce qui a principalement alimenté cette transformation, c'est le boom des gourmets qu'a connu le Japon dans les années 1990, provoqué par l'engouement populaire soudain pour la cuisine italienne. Bien sûr il existait déjà beaucoup d'établissements proposant à Tokyo une cuisine internationale de qualité, sans parler des restaurants japonais chics en place depuis longtemps, mais ils étaient trop peu nombreux pour répondre à la demande générale du public. Il est désormais possible de consommer le type de plats et d'ingrédients sophistiqués que seuls les restaurants japonais de classe supérieure proposaient jusqu'alors. Pour un prix raisonnable vous trouvez maintenant facilement une cuisine internationale non japonisée, mais aussi diverses cuisines métissées, comme dans le Bape Café!? qui offre des plats japonais créatifs, particulièrement populaires chez les jeunes.

Tokyo est devenue une métropole de la restauration au même titre que New York, évolution qui se traduit aussi dans les intérieurs toujours plus stylisés des établissements de restauration. La ville est un lieu de diversification et de fusion de différentes tendances et créé un nouveau style qui lui est propre. Le design japonais typique est revisité selon une perspective européenne occidentale permettant aux designers de réinventer une variété de styles japonais. Les exemples réussis d'un tel renouvellement sont Oto Oto, Daidaiya, Cube Zen, Naka Naka, Zipang etc.

Les designers du Japon, ou d'ailleurs, trouvent l'inspiration dans le « Nouveau Japonisme » qui déferle sur Tokyo pour mener le design sur des chemins inexplorés. Ils découvrent de nouveaux styles et créent un vocabulaire nouveau du design, comme vous le constaterez dans ce livre.

En attirant l'attention sur le raffinement de l'environnement dans la restauration, ces intérieurs magnifiques ne peuvent qu'enrichir l'expérience gastronomique, créant un mariage artistique vibrant qui s'empare du tout Tokyo.

Masaaki Takahishi

Introducción

La calidad de los restaurantes, bares y cafés japoneses ha mejorado considerablemente en las dos últimas décadas, entre otras cosas en lo referente a la comida y mobiliario.

En los años noventa, la escalada de popularidad de la comida italiana disparó en Japón un boom gastronómico que introdujo este cambio en su mayor parte. Obviamente, en numerosos restaurantes de Tokio ya se ofrecía cocina internacional refinada antes de producirse este boom, por no hablar de los excelentes restaurantes japoneses que existían desde hace tiempo, pero su número era demasiado reducido para satisfacer la demanda general. Sin embargo, hoy es posible disfrutar de los refinados ingredientes y platos que antes sólo podían saborearse en los restaurantes de primera categoría de cocina japonesa. En la actualidad, no sólo pueden encontrarse restaurantes de cocina internacional no japonesa a precios razonables, sino también una selección de las denominadas "cocinas mixtas", como p. ej. el ¿¡Café Bape!?, que ofrece platos japoneses creativos que son muy populares entre los clientes jóvenes especialmente.

Tokio se ha convertido en una metrópoli gastronómica que no le va a la zaga a Nueva York. Esta evolución se refleja también en el mobiliario de los establecimientos gastronómicos, cada vez más sofisticado. La ciudad experimenta un cambio y una fusión de diferentes estilos, con lo que se origina un estilo propio totalmente nuevo. El típico diseño japonés recibe una nueva interpretación desde la perspectiva de Europa occidental, con lo que permite a los diseñadores crear variaciones de múltiples estilos japoneses. Oto Oto, Daidaiya, Cube Zen, Naka Naka, Zipang, etc. son buenos ejemplos de este nuevo estilo.

Los diseñadores japoneses y extranjeros encuentran inspiración en un estilo que se extiende de forma imparable: "Japonismo de nuevo género", el cual reorienta el diseño de Tokio en nuevas direcciones. Actualmente se descubren nuevos estilos y nuevos vocabularios de diseño, que también podrá encontrar en este libro.

La atención se centra en un entorno agradable, y así se complementan este mobiliario atractivo y la experiencia gastronómica para desembocar en una fusión artística viva que puede encontrarse en toda la ciudad de Tokio.

Masaaki Takahishi

Introduzione

Negli ultimi due decenni il miglioramento qualitativo dei ristoranti, dei bar e delle caffetterie in Giappone è andato oltre ogni riconoscimento sia per quanto riguarda la cucina che gli interni.

Ciò che ha fatto strada in prima linea a questo mutamento è stato il boom dei gourmet di cui è stato preso il Giappone negli anni novanta, un boom innescato da una improvvisamente accresciuta popolarità della cucina italiana. Naturalmente a Tokyo molte attività offrivano una ristorazione internazionale elaborata anche prima del boom, per non parlare dell'esistenza di ristoranti giapponesi di alto livello e di vecchia tradizione. Tuttavia il loro numero non era sufficiente per soddisfare le esigenze di un grande pubblico. Nel frattempo è reperibile un tipo di ingredienti e di piatti sofisticati che precedentemente poteva solo essere apprezzato in ristoranti elevati di stampo giapponese. Si trovano facilmente per prezzi ragionevoli non solo pietanze internazionali non "giapponizzate" ma anche una varietà di fusion cuisine come per esempio al Bape Cafe!? con i suoi piatti creativi giapponesi che sono venuti in voga soprattutto tra i giovani.

Tokyo è diventata una capitale del "dining out" pari a New York, si tratta di uno sviluppo che si riflette anche negli interni dei locali sempre più stylish. La città sta vivendo una diversificazione e fusione di diversi stili facendo nascere un nuovo stile per sé. Il tipico design giapponese viene reinterpretato in una prospettiva dell'Europa occidentale permettendo ai designers di creare una grande varietà di stili giapponesi. Si trovano numerosi esempi di tale nuovo stile all'Oto Oto, al Daidaiya, al Cube Zen, al Naka Naka, al Zipang ecc.

Il "Nuovo Giapponismo" onnipresente a Tokyo per i designers del posto e dall'estero rappresenta uno stimolo per portare il design in nuove direzioni. Come potrete vedere in questo libro i designers stanno scoprendo nuovi stili e stanno creando un nuovo linguaggio del design.

Prestando attenzione alla raffinatezza e alla bellezza degli interni questi ultimi servono ulteriormente a completare l'esperienza gastronomica creando una vivace sintonia artistica avvertibile in tutta Tokyo.

Masaaki Takahishi

Asli

Design: Naoki Takeda

B1F, New Tokyo Bldg., 3-3-1 Marunouchi | 100-0005 Chiyoda-ku
Phone: +81 3 52 20 55 88
www.wondertable.com | info@wondertable.com
Subway: Yurakucho
Opening hours: Mon–Fri 11:30 am to 3 pm, 5 pm to 11 pm,
Sat–Sun 5 pm to 10 pm
Average price: ¥ 5000
Cuisine: Slow dining

Bamboo Bar

Design: David Rockwell Group

5F, West Walk, Roppongi Hills, 6-10-1 Roppongi | 106-0032 Minato-ku
Phone: +81 3 54 13 95 77
www.soho-s.co.jp
Subway: Roppongi
Opening hours: Mon–Wed 11 am to 11:30 pm, Thu–Sat 11 am to 4 am,
Sun and on holiday 11 am to 23:30 pm
Menu price: Lunch ¥ 1200, Dinner ¥ 3500
Cuisine: International

Seafood Salad

Meeresfrüchtesalat
Salade de fruits de mer
Ensalada de marisco
Insalata di frutti di mare

12 shrimps
12 mussels
4 clams
2 squids
4 scallops
1 carrot
1 celery
1 onion
2 laurel leaves
1 lemon without peel
1 tsp black pepper, crushed
Salt
1 l water

5 tbsp red wine vinegar
Salt, pepper
3 tbsp olive oil
Fresh herbs
1 tomato, diced

Wash sea fruits, cut vegetables in cubes.
Combine all ingredients in a pot and bring to a
boil. Cool in liquid. Take the seafood out of the
fond and peel.
Make a vinaigrette from the last ingredients and
marinate the seafood in it. Garnish with lettuce.

12 Shrimps
12 Miesmuscheln
4 Venusmuscheln
2 Tintenfische
4 Jakobsmuscheln
1 Karotte
1 Sellerie
1 Zwiebel
2 Lorbeerblätter
1 Zitrone ohne Schale
1 TL schwarzer Pfeffer, zerstoßen
Salz
1 l Wasser

5 EL Rotweinessig
Salz, Pfeffer
3 EL Olivenöl
Frische Kräuter der Saison
1 Tomate, gewürfelt

Meeresfrüchte waschen, das Gemüse in Würfel
schneiden. Alle Zutaten in einen Topf geben und
zum Kochen bringen. In der Brühe auskühlen lassen. Die Meeresfrüchte aus dem Fond nehmen
und alle Schalen entfernen.
Aus den übrigen Zutaten eine Vinaigrette zuberei-
ten und die Meeresfrüchte darin marinieren.
Eventuell mit einigen Salatblättern garnieren.

12 crevettes
12 moules
4 palourdes
2 seiches
4 coquilles St. Jacques
1 carotte
1 céleri
1 oignon
2 feuilles de laurier
1 citron sans zeste
1 c. à café de poivre noir moulu
Sel
1 l d'eau

5 c. à soupe de vinaigre de vin rouge
Sel, poivre
3 c. à soupe d'huile d'olive
Herbes fraîches de saison
1 tomate, coupée en dés

Lavez les fruits de mer, découpez les légumes en dés. Versez tous les ingrédients dans une casserole et portez à ébullition. Laissez refroidir dans le bouillon. Retirez les fruits de mer du fond et enlevez toutes les coquilles.
Préparez une vinaigrette avec les ingrédients restants, puis laissez mariner les fruits de mer dedans. Vous pouvez éventuellement garnir le plat de quelques feuilles de salade.

12 gambas
12 mejillones
4 almejas
2 calamares
4 vieiras
1 zanahoria
1 apio
1 cebolla
2 hojas de laurel
1 limón sin corteza
1 cucharadita de pimienta negra, machacada
Sal
1 l de agua

5 cucharadas de vinagre de vino tinto
Sal, pimienta
3 cucharadas de aceite de oliva
Hierbas frescas de temporada
1 tomate, cortado en cuadraditos

Lavar el marisco y cortar la verdura en cuadraditos. Introducir todos los ingredientes en un cazo y poner a hervir. Dejar enfriar en el caldo, sacar el marisco y quitar todas las cáscaras.
Preparar una vinagreta con el resto de los ingredientes y poner el marisco a macerar en la misma. Si se desea, decorar con algunas hojas de lechuga.

12 gamberetti
12 cozze
4 vongole
2 seppie
4 capesante
1 carota
1 costa di sedano
1 cipolla
2 fogli d'alloro
1 limone senza scorza
1 cucchiaino di pepe nero frantumato
Sale
1 l d'acqua

5 cucchiai di aceto di vino rosso
Sale, pepe
3 cucchiai d'olio d'oliva
Erbe fresche stagionali
1 pomodoro tagliato a dadini

Lavate i frutti di mare, tagliate le verdure a dadini. Mettete tutti gli ingredienti in una pentola e fateli cuocere. Fate raffredare nel brodo stesso. Togliete i frutti di mare dal fondo di cottura e sgusciateli.
Preparate con i restanti ingredienti una vinaigrette nella quale marinate i frutti di mare. Decorate eventualmente con fogli di insalata.

Bandol Wine Bar & Restaurant

Design: Lalie Choffel | Chef: Michard David

2F, Ishizuka Shoji Bldg., 2-12-16 Minami-Aoyama | 107-0062 Minato-ku
Phone: +81 3 57 85 37 22
www.bandol-tokyo.com
Subway: Gaienmae, Aoyama 1-Chome
Opening hours: Mon–Fri 6 pm to 2 am, Sat–Sun 12 noon to 3 pm, 6 pm to 2 am
Menu price: Lunch ¥ 3000, Dinner ¥ 5000
Cuisine: French Mediterranean

Bape Café!?

Design: Wonderwall Masamichi Katayama

B1F, 5-3-18 Minami-Aoyama | 107-0062 Minato-ku
Phone: +81 3 57 78 97 26
Subway: Omotesando
Opening hours: Every day 12 noon to 3 pm, 4 pm to 8 pm
Menu price: Lunch ¥ 1000, Dinner ¥ 2000
Cuisine: Asian, American

Tower's Restaurant
Coucagno

Design: Kanto Kikaku Sekkeisha in Association
Chef: Toshinori Sogabe

26-1, Sakuragaoka-cho | 150-8512 Shibuya-ku
Phone: +81 3 34 76 30 00
www.cerulean.panpacific.com
Subway: Shibuya
Opening hours: Lunch 11:30 am to 2 pm, Dinner 5:30 pm to 10 pm
Average price: ¥ 6800
Cuisine: Modern

Tower's Restaurant Coucagno

Cube Zen

Design: Yasuhiro Harada | Chef: Kita

1F, Gate Square Bldg., 5-2-14 Jingumae | 150-0001 Shibuya-ku
Phone: +81 3 54 64 33 31
www.cu-be.com | info@cube-inc.com
Subway: Omotesando
Opening hours: Mon–Fri 11:30 am to 4:30 pm, Sat–Sun 11:30 am to 5:30 pm,
Sun–Thu 6 pm to 11 pm, Fri–Sat 6 pm to 12 midnight
Menu price: Lunch ¥ 1000, Dinner ¥ 3500
Cuisine: Japanese

Chocolate Mousse

with Orange

Schokoladenmousse mit Orange
Mousse au chocolat avec l'orange
Chocolate con naranja
Cioccolata con arancia

3 1/2 oz dark chocolate
200 ml fresh cream
2 tbsp orange marmelade
3 tbsp Grand Marnier
Fruits of the season
Mint leaves

Put the chocolate in a bowl and melt on a hot water bath. Heat half of the cream with Grand Marnier up to 100 °F. Stir in marmelade. Then mix the warm cream with melted chocolate. Chill. Beat the leftover cold cream until it becomes half stiff. Carefully fold the whipped cream under the cream-chocolate mixture. Put mousse into four coffeepots and chill in the fridge for two hours. Put cups on saucers and decorate with fruits and mint leaves.

100 g Bitterschokolade
200 ml Sahne
2 EL Orangenmarmelade
3 EL Grand Marnier
Früchte der Saison
Minze

Schokolade in einem Wasserbad schmelzen. Die Hälfte der Sahne mit dem Grand Marnier auf ca. 40 °C erhitzen. Marmelade einrühren. Nun die warme Sahne mit der Schokolade vermischen. Abkühlen lassen. Die restliche Sahne halbfest schlagen und vorsichtig unter die abgekühlte Schoko-Sahne heben. Die Masse in vier Kaffeetassen verteilen und zwei Stunden kaltstellen. Die Tassen auf Untertassen stellen und mit Früchten und Minze garnieren.

100 g de chocolat amer
200 ml de crème
2 c. à soupe de marmelade d'orange
3 c. à soupe de Grand Marnier
Fruits de saison
Menthe

Faites fondre le chocolat au bain-marie. Chauffez la moitié de la crème à 40 °C environ avec le Grand Marnier. Incorporez la marmelade. Mélangez ensuite la crème chaude avec le chocolat. Laissez refroidir. Battre le reste de crème jusqu'à une consistance semi-épaisse et incorporez-la doucement à la crème au chocolat refroidie. Répartissez le tout dans quatre tasses à café et réservez au froid pendant deux heures. Disposez les tasses sur des soucoupes et garnissez-les de fruits et de menthe.

100 g de chocolate amargo
200 ml de nata
2 cucharadas de mermelada de naranja
3 cucharadas de Grand Marnier
Frutas del tiempo
Menta

Deshacer el chocolate al baño María. Calentar la mitad de la nata con el Grand Marnier a aprox. 40 °C . Incorporar la mermelada. A continuación mezclar la nata caliente con el chocolate y dejar enfriar. Batir la nata restante hasta que esté cremosa y agregar cuidadosamente a la mezcla enfriada de chocolate y nata. Distribuir la masa en cuatro tazas de café y poner a enfriar durante dos horas. Colocar las tazas sobre los platillos y decorar con las frutas y la menta.

100 g di cioccolato amara
200 ml di panna
2 cucchiai di marmellata di arance
3 cucchiai di Grand Marnier
Frutta della stagione
Menta

Fate fondere la cioccolato a bagnomaria. Riscaldate la metà della panna insieme con il Grand Marnier fino a una temperatura di circa 40 °C. Aggiungete la marmellata mescolando, quindi mescolare la panna riscaldata con la cioccolato e lasciate raffreddare. Montate leggermente la panna restante e fatela integrarsi con cura nell'amalgama di panna e cioccolata raffreddato. Distribuite il tutto in quattro tazze da tè e fate raffreddare per due ore. Mettete le tazze sui piattini e guarnite con frutta e menta.

Daidaiya

Design: Hasimoto Yukio Design Studio | Chef: Kenichiro Fujita

2F, Ginza Nine 1 Goukan, 8-5 Saki, Ginza | 104-0061 Chuo-ku
Phone: +81 3 55 37 35 66
www.chanto.com
Subway: Shinbashi
Opening hours: Mon–Sun 5 pm to 1 am, Fri 5 pm to 4 am
Average price: ¥ 5000
Cuisine: New Japanese

Sushi

4 shrimps
Salt
4 tsp Miso paste

3 1/2 oz tuna
2 tbsp soy sauce
Bonito flakes

3 1/2 oz Menegi-tuna
4 quail eggs, boiled
Bonito flakes
4 leaves of seaweed (Nori)

Peony Shrimps
Wash, dry and remove black back line of each shrimp. Leave last tailpiece. Season. Garnish with Miso paste.

Raw tuna with Tosa Shoyu
Cut tuna in four thick slices. Mix soy sauce with dried bonito flakes to make a thick creme. Spoon creme on tuna.

Menegi-tuna with quail egg
Cut Menegi-tuna in four slices. Sprinkle each piece with bonito flakes, top with cooked quail egg and wrap in a leave of seaweed.

4 Garnelen
Salz
4 TL Misopaste

100 g Thunfisch
2 EL Sojasauce
Bonito-Flocken

100 g Menegi-Thunfisch
4 Wachteleier, hart gekocht
Bonito-Flocken
4 Blatt Seetang (Nori)

Pfingstrosen-Garnelen
Garnelen waschen, trockentupfen, auf einer Seite aufschneiden und Darm entfernen. Das letzte Schwanzglied dranlassen. Salzen. Mit Misopaste garnieren.

Roher Thunfisch mit Tosa Shoyu
Thunfisch in vier dicke Scheiben schneiden. Sojasauce mit getrockneten Bonito-Flocken vermischen bis eine dicke Paste entsteht. Paste auf den Thunfisch streichen.

Menegi-Thunfisch mit Wachtelei
Menegi-Thunfisch in vier Scheiben schneiden. Jedes Stück mit Bonito-Flocken bestreuen und mit einem gekochten Wachtelei in ein Blatt Seetang einwickeln.

4 crevettes
Sel
4 c. à café de pâte miso

100 g de thon
2 c. à soupe de sauce au soja
Flocons de bonite

100 g de thon menegi
4 œufs de caille, dur
Flocons de bonite
4 feuilles d'algue séchée

Crevettes pivoine
Lavez les crevettes, séchez-les en les tamponnant, ouvrez-les sur un côté, puis retirez les intestins. Laissez le dernier segment de la queue. Salez. Garnissez de pâte miso.

Thon cru au Tosa Shoyu
Coupez le thon en quatre tranches épaisses. Mélangez la sauce au soja avec les flocons séchés de bonite jusqu'à obtenir une pâte épaisse. Etalez la pâte sur le thon.

Thon menegi aux oeufs de caille
Coupez le thon menegi en quatre tranches. Saupoudrez chaque tranche avec des flocons de bonite et enroulez-le avec un œuf de caille cuit dans une feuille d'algue séchée.

---

4 gambas de flor de peonía
Sal
4 cucharaditas de pasta de miso

100 g de atún
2 cucharadas de salsa de soja
Copos de bonito

100 g de atún Menegi
4 huevos de codorniz cocidos
Copos de bonito
4 hojas d'algas marinas

Gambas de flor de peonía
Lavar las gambas, secar dando unos toques con papel de cocina y hacerles una incisión a lo largo extrayéndoles el intestino. Dejar la última articulación de la cola. Sazonar. Decorar con pasta de miso.

Atún crudo con Tosa Shoyu
Cortar el atún en cuatro lonchas gruesas. Mezclar la salsa de soja con los copos de bonito hasta que se forme una pasta gruesa. Untar el atún con la pasta.

Atún Menegi con huevo de codorniz
Cortar el atún Menegi en cuatro lonchas. Esparcir copos de bonito sobre cada loncha y envolver en una hoja d'algas marinas junto con un huevo de codorniz cocido.

---

4 gamberi bianchi
Sale
4 cucchiaino di Miso (pasta di soia fermentata)

100 g di tonno
2 cucchiai di salsa di soia
Fiocchi di bonito

100 g di tonno menegi
4 uova di quaglia sodo
Fiocchi di bonito
4 fogli d'alga marina

Gamberi bianchi
Lavate i gamberi, asciugateli, apriteli da un lato ed eliminatene le interiora lasciando l'ultima parte dei carapaci e la coda. Regolate di sale e guarnite con miso.

Tonno crudo con tosa shoyu (salsa di soia)
Tagliare il tonno a quattro fette grosse. Mescolare la salsa di soia con i fiocchi di bonito seccati in modo da creare una crema densa. Spalmare la crema sul tonno.

Tonno menegi con uovo di quaglia
Tagliare il tonno menegi a quattro fette. Cospargere ogni fetta con fiocchi di bonito e avvolgerle insieme con un uovo di quaglia sodo in un foglio d'alga marina.

Ginto

Design: Yasumichi Morita

4F, Minami Ikebukuro Kyoudou Bldg., 1-19-5 Minami Ikebukuro | 171-0022 Toshima-ku
Phone: +81 3 39 80 08 00
www.ginto.jp
Subway: Ikebukuro
Opening hours: Mon–Fri Lunch 11:30 am to 5 pm, Dinner 5 pm to 10:30 pm,
Sat–Sun Dinner 5 pm to 11 pm
Menu price: Lunch ¥ 2000, Dinner ¥ 5000
Cuisine: French

Hajime

Design: Yasumichi Morita GLAMOROUS CO. Ltd.
Chef: Hajime Machida

B1F, Iraka Ginza Bldg., 6-4-7 Ginza | 104-0061 Chuo-ku
Phone: +81 3 55 68 45 52
www.ginza-hajime.com
Subway: Ginza
Opening hours: Mon–Fri 6 pm to 3 am, Sat 6 pm to 11 pm, closed on Sunday
Average price: ¥ 6000–7000

If

Design: Claudio Colucci Design / R.B.S.

1F, J-Park Ebisu 4 Bankan, 3-2-5 Ebisu | 150-0013 Shibuya-ku
Phone: +81 3 57 39 08 48
www.foodworks.jp
Subway: Ebisu
Opening hours: Every day 11:30 am to 2 pm, 5 pm to 11 pm
Menu price: Lunch ¥ 900, Dinner ¥ 4000
Cuisine: Italian

Linguine

with Basil Paste and Shrimps

Linguine mit Pesto und Garnelen
Linguine au pesto et aux crevettes
Linguine con pesto y langostinos
Linguine con pesto e gamberoni

2 bunches basil
2 tbsp Parmesan cheese
2 tbsp roasted pine nuts
Olive oil as needed
Salt, pepper

8 king prawns
8 cherry tomatoes
approx. 3 1/2 oz green beans
1 spring onion
1 small carrot
2 tbsp olive oil
Salt, pepper
7 oz thin spaghetti

Combine basil leaves, Parmesan cheese, pine nuts and olive oil in a blender and mix until smooth.
Clean the prawns and remove black back line. Wash vegetables, then cut tomatoes in half, peel carrot and cut in slices, cut off ends of beans, perhaps remove stringy parts. Cut spring onion in rings.
Heat olive oil in a pan and fry shrimps, add vegetables except tomatoes and sauté on low heat. At the end add tomatoes and season for taste.
Cook spaghetti al dente, mix with basil paste and place on a plate, top with shrimps and vegetables.

2 Bund Basilikum
2 EL Parmesan
2 EL geröstete Pinienkerne
Olivenöl nach Bedarf
Salz, Pfeffer

8 Riesengarnelen
8 Kirschtomaten
ca. 100 g grüne Stangenbohnen
1 Frühlingszwiebel
1 kleine Karotte
2 EL Olivenöl
Salz, Pfeffer
200 g Spaghettini

Die Basilikumblätter mit dem Parmesan, den Pinienkernen und dem Olivenöl in einem Mixer pürieren und abschmecken.
Die Garnelen putzen und den Darm entfernen. Das Gemüse waschen, dann die Tomaten halbieren, die Karotte schälen und in Scheiben schneiden, die Enden der Bohnen abschneiden und evtl. die Fäden entfernen. Die Frühlingszwiebel in Ringe schneiden.
Olivenöl in einer Pfanne erhitzen und die Garnelen scharf anbraten, das Gemüse außer den Tomaten hinzufügen und auf kleiner Flamme garen. Die Tomaten zum Schluss zugeben und abschmecken.
Spaghettini al dente kochen, mit dem Pesto mischen, auf einem Teller anrichten und das Garnelengemüse darüber geben.

2 bouquets de basilic
2 c. à soupe de parmesan
2 c. à soupe de pignons de pin grillés
Huile d'olive à volonté
Sel, poivre

8 gambas
8 tomates-cerises
100 g env. d'haricots verts à rames
1 oignon printanier
1 petite carotte
2 c. à soupe d'huile d'olive
Sel, poivre
200 g spaghettini

Pour le pesto, réduisez en purée les feuilles de basilic, le parmesan, les pignons de pin et l'huile d'olive dans un mixeur et assaisonnez à votre goût.
Décortiquez les gambas et retirez les intestins.
Lavez les légumes, puis coupez les tomates en deux, coupez la carotte en tranches, équeutez les haricots et enlevez éventuellement les fils.
Coupez l'oignon printanier en rondelles.
Faites chauffer de l'huile d'olive dans une poêle et saisissez les gambas, ajoutez-y les légumes à l'exception des tomates et faites cuire à feux doux. Ajoutez les tomates en fin de cuisson et assaisonnez à votre goût.
Cuisez les spaghettinis al dente, mélangez-les au pesto, disposez le tout dans une assiette et ajoutez-y la poêlée de légumes et de gambas.

2 ramilletes de albahaca
2 cucharadas de parmesano
2 cucharadas de piñones tostados
Aceite de oliva al gusto
Sal, pimienta

8 langostinos
8 tomates tipo "cherry"
Aprox. 100 g de judías verdes
1 cebolleta
1 zanahoria pequeña
2 cucharadas de aceite de oliva
Sal, pimienta
200 g de spaghettini

Para el pesto triturar las hojas de albahaca, el parmesano, los piñones y el aceite de oliva con la batidora y aderezar al gusto.
Limpiar los langostinos, extrayéndoles el intestino. Lavar la verdura, después partir los tomates por la mitad, cortar la zanahoria en lonchas y los extremos de las judías verdes, retirando los hilos si los hubiera. Cortar la cebolleta en anillos.
Calentar el aceite de oliva en una sartén y freír los langostinos a fuego fuerte. Añadir la verdura, excepto los tomates, y dejar cocer a fuego lento.
Añadir por último los tomates y aderezar al gusto.
Cocer los spaghettini al dente y mezclarlos con el pesto. Servir en un plato y cubrir con la verdura y los langostinos.

2 mazzetti di basilico
2 cucchiai di parmigiano
2 cucchiai di pinoli tostati
Olio d'oliva a volontà
Sale, pepe

8 gamberoni
8 pomodorini
circa 100 g di fagioli verdi rampicanti
1 cipollotto
1 carota piccola
2 cucchiai d'olio d'oliva
Sale, pepe
200 g di spaghettini

Per ottenere il pesto, frullate le foglie di basilico con il parmigiano, i pinoli e l'olio d'oliva e insaporitelo.
Pulire i gamberoni e eliminare le interiora. Lavare la verdura, quindi tagliare a metà i pomodori, tagliare la carota a dischetti, eliminare le estremità ed eventualmente il filo dei fagiolini. Tagliare il cipollotto a cerchietti.
Rosolare i gamberoni in padella nell'olio d'oliva bollente, unire la verdura tranne i pomodori e fare cuocere a fiamma lenta. Aggiungere alla fine i pomodori e insaporire.
Cuocere gli spaghettini al dente, mescolare con il pesto, disporre su un piatto e mettere la verdura e i gamberoni sopra.

Ken's Dining

Design: Yasumichi Morita | Chef: Toshiaki Abe

B1F, FF Bldg., 3-26-6 Shinjuku | 160-0022 Shinjuku-ku
Phone: +81 3 53 63 03 36
www.chanto.com
Subway: Shinjuku
Opening hours: Every day 11:30 am to 1 am
Menu price: Lunch ¥ 1200, Dinner ¥ 5000
Cuisine: Japanese

Tofu-Cheese-Antipasti

Tofukäse-Antipasti

Entrée de fromage au tofu

Antipasto de queso de tofu

Antipasti al formaggio di tofu

10 1/2 oz cream cheese
100 ml soy milk
3 leaves gelatine
1 pinch salt

Toppings:
2 tbsp caviar
2 tbsp diced tomatoes
Olives or olive paste (Tapenade)
Wasabi (Japanese horse radish)
Fresh herbs

Soak gelatine in cold water. Warm the cream cheese. Heat up the soy milk and dissolve the soaked gelatine in it. Mix cream cheese and soy milk and season with salt. Chill, until the cream cheese thickens. Pour into a flat, square tray and put in the fridge (approx. 4–5 hours). Then cut in square pieces, place on plates or spoons and decorate with toppings.

300 g Frischkäse
100 ml Sojamilch
3 Blatt Gelatine
1 Prise Salz

Garnitur:
2 EL Kaviar
2 EL Tomatenwürfel
Oliven oder Olivenpaste (Tapenade)
Wasabi (japanischer Meerrettich)
Frische Kräuter

Die Gelatine in kaltem Wasser einweichen. Den Frischkäse leicht erwärmen. Die Sojamilch erhitzen und die ausgedrückte Gelatine darin auflösen. Frischkäse und Sojamilch miteinander mischen und abschmecken. Auskühlen lassen bis die Masse anfängt zu stocken. In eine flache eckige Form geben und im Kühlschrank fest werden lassen (ca. 4–5 Stunden). Nun in Rechtecke schneiden und auf Tellern oder Löffeln anrichten. Garnieren.

300 g de fromage frais
100 ml de lait de soja
3 feuilles de gélatine
1 pincée de sel

Garniture :
2 c. à soupe de caviar
2 c. à soupe de dés de tomate
Olives ou tapenade
Wasabi (sorte de raifort japonais)
Herbes fraîches

Faites ramollir la gélatine dans de l'eau froide. Réchauffez légèrement le fromage frais. Faites chauffer le lait de soja et dissolvez-y la gélatine écrasée. Mélangez le fromage frais et le lait de soja et assaisonnez à votre goût. Laissez refroidir jusqu'à ce que le tout commence à se rigidifier. Versez dans un moule angulaire à fond plat et laissez prendre au réfrigérateur (environ 4–5 heures). Découpez ensuite en rectangles et disposez-les sur des assiettes ou dans des cuillères. Garnissez.

---

300 g de queso fresco
100 ml de leche de soja
3 hojas de gelatina
1 pizca de sal

Guarnición:
2 cucharadas de caviar
2 cucharadas de tomates cortados en cuadraditos
Aceitunas o pasta de aceitunas (tapenade)
Wasabi (rabanete japonés)
Hierbas frescas

Poner en remojo la gelatina en agua fría. Calentar ligeramente el queso fresco. Calentar la leche de soja y disolver en la misma la gelatina escurrida. Mezclar el queso fresco y la leche de soja y aderezar al gusto. Dejar enfriar hasta que la masa comience a cuajar. Introducir en un molde plano y cuadrangular y dejar solidificar en el frigorífico (aprox. 4–5 horas). A continuación cortar en rectángulos y servir sobre un plato o una cuchara. Decorar.

---

300 g di formaggio di latte cagliato
100 ml di latte di soia
3 fogli di gelatina
1 pizzico di sale

Guarnizione:
2 cucchiai di caviale
2 cucchiai di pomodori tagliati a dadini
Olive o pesto d'olive
Wasabi (radice giapponese)
Erbe fresche

Mettete a bagno la gelatina in acqua fredda. Intiepidite il formaggio di latte cagliato. Riscaldate il latte di soia e scioglietevi la gelatina asciugata. Mescolate il formaggio di latte cagliato ed il latte di soia e insaporite. Lasciate raffreddare finché il composto inizi a rapprendersi. Versate in un recipiente rettangolare basso e lasciate addensare in frigo (per circa 4–5 ore). Ora, tagliare a rettangoli e disporre su piatti o cucchiai. Guarnire.

La Fabrique

Design: Junpei Yamaiwa (Myu Planning & Operators Inc.)

B1F, Zero-Gate Bldg., 16-9 Udawaga-cho | 150-0042 Shibuya-ku
Phone: +81 3 5 42 85 20
www.lafabrique.jp
Subway: Shibuya
Opening hours: Lunch every day 11 am to 6 pm,
Dinner Mon–Thu 6 pm to 2 am, Fri–Sun 6 pm to 11 pm
Average price: ¥ 4000
Cuisine: Casual French

Las Chicas

Design: Mr. VO | Chef: Tony Schimonello

5-47-6 Jingumae | 150-0001 Shibuya-ku
Phone: +81 3 34 07 68 65
www.vision.co.jp
Subway: Omotesando
Opening hours: Mon–Fri 11 am to 11 pm, Sat–Sun 11 am to 11:30 pm
Menu price: Lunch ¥ 1500, Dinner ¥ 3500
Cuisine: Modern Australian

Seared Scallops

with Avocado and Tomato on Basil Oil

Gebratene Jakobsmuscheln mit Avocado und Tomate an Basilikumöl

Coquilles St. Jacques cuites à l'avocat et à la tomate et son filet d'huile au basilic

Vieiras fritas con aguacate, tomate y aceite de albahaca

Capesante saltate con avocado, pomodori e olio al basilico

3 oz basil
1 glove of garlic
Juice of half a lemon
Salt, pepper
100 ml olive oil

12 scallops, without shell
1 avocado
Juice of a lemon
2 tomatoes
Salt, pepper
Tabasco
Lettuce for decoration

Combine first six ingredients in a blender and mix until smooth. Chill.
Peel avocado and cut in squares. Marinate with lemon juice, salt and pepper. Skin tomatoes, discard seeds, dice and season with salt, pepper and Tabasco. Season scallops and fry in a hot pan with olive oil for about two minutes each side. Divide avocado and tomatoes on four plates, put scallops around them and garnish with basil oil and lettuce.

80 g Basilikum
1 Knoblauchzehe
Saft einer halben Zitrone
Salz, Pfeffer
100 ml Olivenöl

12 Jakobsmuscheln, ohne Schale
1 Avocado
Saft einer Zitrone
2 Tomaten
Salz, Pfeffer
Tabasco
Salatblätter zum Dekorieren

Die ersten sechs Zutaten in einen Mixer geben und fein pürieren. Kaltstellen.
Avocado schälen und in grobe Stücke schneiden. Mit Zitronensaft, Salz und Pfeffer marinieren. Tomaten abziehen, die Kerne entfernen, in Würfel schneiden und mit Salz, Pfeffer und Tabasco würzen. Die Jakobsmuscheln würzen und in heißem Olivenöl auf jeder Seite ca. zwei Minuten braten. Tomaten und Avocado auf vier Tellern verteilen, die Jakobsmuscheln darum setzen, mit Basilikumöl und Salatblättern dekorieren.

80 g de basilic
1 gousse d'ail
Jus d'un demi-citron
Sel, poivre
100 ml d'huile d'olive

12 coquilles St. Jacques, sans coquille
1 avocat
Jus d'un citron
2 tomates
Sel, poivre
Tabasco
Feuilles de salade pour la décoration

Mettez les six premiers ingrédients dans un mixeur et réduisez le tout en purée. Réservez au froid. Pelez l'avocat et découpez-le en gros morceaux. Faites-les mariner dans le jus de citron, avec du sel et du poivre. Pelez les tomates, épépinez-les et découpez-les en dés, puis assaisonnez-les à votre goût avec du sel, du poivre et du tabasco. Assaisonnez à votre goût les coquilles St. Jacques et cuisez-les deux minutes environ de chaque côté dans de l'huile d'olive chaude. Répartissez les tomates et l'avocat dans quatre assiettes, disposez autour les coquilles St. Jacques, puis décorez avec l'huile au basilic et les feuilles de salade.

80 g de albahaca
1 diente de ajo
Jugo de medio limón
Sal, pimienta
100 ml de aceite de oliva

12 vieiras, sin concha
1 aguacate
Jugo de un limón
2 tomates
Sal, pimienta
Tabasco
Hojas de lechuga para decorar

Introducir los primeros seis ingredientes en una batidora y triturar hasta hacer un puré fino. Poner a enfriar. Pelar el aguacate y cortar en trozos gruesos. Marinar en jugo de limón, sal y pimienta. Pelar los tomates, quitar las pepitas, cortar en cuadraditos y condimentar con sal, pimienta y tabasco. Condimentar las vieiras y freír en aceite de oliva caliente durante aprox. dos minutos por cada lado. Distribuir los tomates y el aguacate en cuatro platos, disponer las vieiras alrededor, decorar con aceite de albahaca y hojas de lechuga.

80 g di basilico
1 spicchio d'aglio
Il succo di mezzo limone
Sale, pepe
100 ml d'olio d'oliva

12 capesante sgusciate
1 avocado
Il succo di un limone
2 pomodori
Sale, pepe
Tabasco
Fogli di insalata per guarnire

Mettere le prima sei ingredienti nel frullatore e ben frullare. Far raffreddare. Sbucciare l'avocado e tagliarlo a pezzi piuttosto grandi. Marinare con succo di limone, sale e pepe. Privare i pomodori della pelle e dei semi, tagliarli a dadini e condire con sale, pepe e tabasco. Condire le capesante e far friggere in olio d'oliva bollente per circa due minuti ambo i lati. Dividere i pomodori e l'avocado su quattro piatti, disporre le capesante intorno a questi e guarnire con l'olio al basilico e fogli di insalata.

Le Cocon

Design: Hideo Horikawa Architect & Associates
Chef: Tadashi Honma

1F, Union Square Bldg., 2-8 Uguisudani-cho | 150-0032 Shibuya-ku
Phone: +81 3 54 59 53 66
Subway: Shibuya
Opening hours: Mon–Wed 6 pm to 11 pm, Tue–Sat 6 pm to 4 am,
closed on Sunday
Average price: ¥ 5000
Cuisine: French

Le Dragon Bleu

Design: Studio Spin (Yasuhiro Koichi, Masakazu Koizumi)

6F, Ginza Namikidori Bldg., 2-3-6 Ginza | 104-0061 Chuo-ku
Phone: +81 3 35 38 22 11
www.soho-s.co.jp
Subway: Yurakucho, Ginza
Opening hours: Every day 11:30 am to 3 pm, 5:30 pm to 11:00 pm,
Sat–Sun 5:30 pm to 4 am
Menu price: Lunch ¥ 1200, Dinner ¥ 4500
Cuisine: Asian

Nama Haru Maki

24 rice papers
1 cucumber
4 steamed chicken breasts
24 cooked shrimps
2 tbsp chili oil
1 tsp dried shrimp powder
Salt, pepper
1 leek

Hot chilli sauce
2 limes

Soak rice paper in water. Cut cucumber and chicken in thin slices. Marinate shrimps in chili oil and season with shrimp powder, salt and pepper. Cook leek until soft.
Take a slice cucumber and chicken, one shrimp and a piece of leek and roll them tight in a rice paper.
Make six rolls for each person, tie with the leftover leek.
Serve with hot chilli sauce and half a lime.

24 Blätter Reispapier
1 Salatgurke
4 gedämpfte Hähnchenbrüste
24 gekochte Shrimps
2 EL Chiliöl
1 TL getrocknetes Shrimpspulver
Salz, Pfeffer
1 Lauch

Scharfe Chilisauce
2 Limonen

Reispapier in Wasser einweichen. Salatgurke und Hähnchen in dünne Scheiben schneiden. Shrimps in Chiliöl einlegen und mit getrocknetem Shrimpspulver, Salz und Pfeffer würzen. Lauch blanchieren.
Jeweils eine Scheibe Gurke und Hähnchen, ein Shrimp und ein Stück Lauch fest in ein Blatt Reispapier einwickeln.
Pro Person sechs Röllchen formen und mit längeren Lauchstreifen zusammenbinden.
Mit scharfer Chilisauce und einer halben Limone servieren.

24 feuilles de papier de riz
1 concombre
4 blancs de poulet cuits à l'étuvée
24 crevettes cuites
2 c. à soupe d'huile au piment
1 c. à café de poudre de crevette sèche
Sel, poivre
1 branche de poireau

Sauce pimentée âcre
2 citrons verts

Faites ramollir le papier de riz dans de l'eau.
Découpez le concombre et le poulet en tranches
fines. Faites baigner les crevettes dans de l'huile
au piment et assaisonnez à votre goût avec la
poudre de crevette sèche, le sel et le poivre.
Faites blanchir le poireau.
Enroulez ensemble bien serrés dans une feuille
de papier de riz une tranche de concombre, une
tranche de poulet, une crevette et un morceau de
poireau.
Préparez six petits rouleaux par personne que
vous assemblerez avec de longues lanières de
poireau.
Servez avec une sauce chili épicée et un demi-
citron vert.

24 hojas de papel de arroz
1 pepino de ensalada
4 pechugas de pollo al vapor
24 gambas cocidas
2 cucharadas de aceite de guindilla
1 cucharadita de polvo de gambas secas
Sal, pimienta
1 puerro

Salsa de guindilla picante
2 limas

Poner el papel de arroz en remojo con agua.
Cortar el pepino de ensalada y el pollo en lonchas
finas. Macerar las gambas en aceite de guindilla
y condimentar con polvo de gambas secas, sal y
pimienta. Hervir ligeramente el puerro.
Envolver en una hoja de papel de arroz una loncha de pepino, otra de pollo, una gamba y un
trozo de puerro, presionando fuertemente.
Formar seis rollitos por persona y atarlos con las
tiras del puerro más largas.
Servir con salsa de guindilla picante y media lima.

24 fogli di carta di riso
1 cetriolo
4 petti di pollo cotti a vapore
24 gamberetti bolliti
2 cucchiai d'olio al chili
1 cucchiaino di polvere di gamberetti essiccati
Sale, pepe
1 porro

Salsa di chili piccante
2 limoni verdi

Mettere a bagno la carta di riso. Tagliare il cetriolo ed il pollo a fette sottili. Mettere i gamberetti
sott'olio di chili e condire con la polvere di gamberetti essiccati, regolare di sale e pepe. Scottare
il porro.
Avvolgere in ciascun foglio di riso una fetta di
cetriolo, una fetta di pollo, un gamberetto e un
pezzo di porro.
Formare sei rotolini a persona e legarli con le
foglie di porro più lunghe.
Servire con salsa di chili piccante e con mezzo
limone verde.

Maimon

Design: Hashimoto Yukio Design Studio Co. Ltd.
Chef: Takenouchi

1F, Fujimizaka-place, 3-17-29 Nishi-Azabu | 106-0031 Minato-ku
Phone: +81 3 34 08 26 00
www.foodscope.co.jp
Subway: Azabu Juban
Opening hours: Mon–Thu 6 pm to 4 am, Fri–Sat 6 pm to 5 am
Average price: ¥ 7000
Cuisine: Oyster Bar & Charcoal Grill

Oyster Shooter

Austern-Shooter
Shooter aux huîtres
Shooter de ostras
Shooter alle ostriche

4 long drink glasses
8 oysters

Sauce 1:
1 Daikon (Japanese radish)
20 ml Ume (plum vinegar)
Salted Konbu, chopped (seaweed)
Grate Daikon and mix with other ingredients.

Sauce 2:
1 potato, cooked
50 ml Ponzu (vinegar with soy sauce and Yuzu
(Japanese lemon))
2 tsp salmon roe
1 tbsp Asatsuki chives, minced
Mash potato and mix with other ingredients.

Sauce 3:
1 oz Tokwa (firm tofu)
2 tbsp Nibaizu (vinegar and soy sauce)
1 tsp Wasabi (Japanese radish)
1 sea-urchin, chopped
Mix all ingredients.

Put two oysters in a glass, put the sauce of your
choice on it and drink.
You can also add champagne, if you like.

4 Longdrink-Gläser
8 Austern

Sauce 1:
1 Daikon (japanischer Rettich)
20 ml Ume (japanischer Pflaumenessig)
Gesalzenes Konbu, gehackt (Seetang, Algen)
Daikon raspeln und mit den anderen Zutaten
mischen.

Sauce 2:
1 Kartoffel, gekocht
50 ml Ponzu (Essig mit Sojasauce und Yuzu (japanische Zitrone))
2 TL Lachsrogen
1 EL Asatsuki-Schnittlauch, fein geschnitten
Kartoffel reiben und mit den anderen Zutaten
mischen.

Sauce 3:
30 g Tokwa (fester Tofu)
2 EL Nibaizu (Essig und Sojasauce)
1 TL Wasabi (japanischer Meerrettich)
1 Seeigel, gehackt
Alle Zutaten mischen.

Zwei Austern in ein Glas geben, mit der Sauce
Ihrer Wahl bedecken und wie einen Schnaps auf
ex trinken.
Nach Wunsch mit Champagner aufgießen.

4 verres à longdrink
8 huîtres

Sauce 1:
1 Daikon (radis japonais)
20 ml d'Ume (vinaigre de prune japonais)
Kombu salé (algues)
Râpez le Daikon et mélangez-le aux autres ingrédients.

Sauce 2:
1 pomme de terre, cuite
50 ml de Ponzu (vinaigre à la sauce soja et Yuzu (citron japonais))
2 c. à soupe de œufs de saumon
1 c. à soupe de ciboulette Asatsuki, finement coupée
Râpez la pomme de terre et mélangez-la aux autres ingrédients.

Sauce 3:
30 g de Tokwa (tofu du)
2 c. à soupe de Nibaizu (vinaigre et sauce soja)
1 c. à café de Wasabi (radis japonais)
1 oursin, haché
Mélangez tous les ingrédients.

Mettez deux huîtres dans un verre, recouvrez de la sauce de votre choix et buvez d'un trait comme une liqueur.
Vous pouvez également arroser de champagne si vous le souhaitez.

---

4 vasos altos
8 ostras

Salsa 1:
1 Daikon (rábano japonés)
20 ml de Ume (vinagre japonés de ciruelas)
Kombu salado, picado (algas marinas, algas)
Rallar el Daikon y mezclar con los demás ingredientes.

Salsa 2:
1 patata cocida
50 ml de Ponzu (vinagre con salsa de soja y Yuzu (limón japonés))
2 cucharaditas de huevas de salmón
1 cucharadas de cebollino (Asatsuki), cortado fino
Rallar la patata y mezclar con los demás ingredientes.

Salsa 3:
30 g de Tokwa (tofu sólido)
2 cucharaditas de Nibaizu (vinagre y salsa de soja)
1 cucharadita de Wasabi (rabanete japonés)
1 erizo de mar, troceado
Mezclar todos los ingredientes.

Introducir dos ostras en una copita, cubrir con la salsa de su elección y beber de golpe como un aguardiente.
Si se desea, rellenar con champán.

---

4 bicchieri da long drink
8 ostriche

Salsa 1:
1 Daikon (rafano bianco giapponese)
20 ml di ume (aceto di prugne giapponese)
Kombu salato, tritati (alga)
Grattugiare il daikon e mescolarlo con gli altri ingredienti.

Salsa 2:
1 patata lessa
50 ml di Ponzu (aceto con salsa di soia e Yuzu (limone giapponese))
2 cucchiai d'uova di salmone
1 cucchiaio di erba cipollina Asatsuki ben tritata
Grattugiare la patata e mescolarla con gli altri ingredienti.

Salsa 3:
30 g di Tokwa (tofu sodo)
2 cucchiai di Nibaizu (aceto e salsa di soia)
1 cucchiaino di Wasabi (radice giapponese)
1 ricci di mare, tritati
Mescolare tutti gli ingredienti.

Mettere due ostriche in un bicchiero, coprirle di una salsa a scelta e bere come una grappa in un sorso.
Irrorare di champagne a volontà.

Naka Naka

Design: Yusaku Kaneshiro

6F, Peace Bldg., 3-34-11 Shinjuku | 160-0022 Shinjuku-ku
Phone: +81 3 53 12 28 45
www.masumoto.co.jp
Subway: Shinjuku
Opening hours: Mon–Sat 5 pm to 12 midnight, Sun and on Holiday 5 pm to 11 pm
Average price: ¥ 5000
Cuisine: Japanese

Nemesis

2F, 4-10-7 Nishi-Azabu | 106-0031 Minato-ku
Phone: +81 3 54 67 16 50
www.bar-nemesis.com | yume@bar-nemesis.com
Subway: Hiroo
Opening hours: Mon–Sat 7 pm to 5 am, closed on Sunday and Holiday
Average price: ¥ 4000

MadameX

30 ml Karuvadosu
10 ml lime juice
10 ml cranberry juice
10 ml Puorokka

Carefully pour all ingredients in a willowy shaped glass, that is suffused in red, beginning with the first liquid.

3 cl Karuvadosu
1 cl Limonensaft
1 cl Preiselbeersaft
1 cl Puorukka

Alle Zutaten nacheinander vorsichtig in ein schlankes Glas geben, das Rot getönt ist. Man beginnt mit der ersten Flüssigkeit.

3 cl de Karuvadosu
1 cl de jus de citron vert
1 cl de jus d'airelle
1 cl de Puorukka

Ajoutez l'un après l'autre tous les ingrédients avec précaution dans un verre étroit, coloré en rouge. Commencez avec le premier liquide.

3 cl de Karuvadosu
1 cl de jugo de lima
1 cl de jugo de arándanos rojos
1 cl de Puorukka

Introducir con cuidado todos los ingredientes uno detrás de otro en un vaso delgado de color rojizo. Se comienza con el primer liquído.

3 cl di Karuvadosu
1 cl di succo di limoni verdi
1 cl di succo di mirtilli rossi
1 cl di Puorukka

Versare attentamente tutti gli ingredienti in un bicchiere stretto di colore rossiccio. Iniziate con il primo liquido.

New York Grill

Design: Kenzo Tange Associates | Chef: Matthew Craebe

3-7-1-2 Nishi-Shinjuku | 163-1055 Shinjuku-ku
Phone: +81 3 53 23 34 58
www.parkhyatttokyo.com
Subway: Shinjuku
Opening hours: Every day Lunch 11:30 am to 2:30 pm, Dinner 5:30 pm to 10:30 pm
Menu price: Lunch ¥ 4800, Dinner ¥ 10000
Cuisine: Contemporary international

NOS

Design: Myu Planning & Operators Inc.

5-10-17 Minami-Aoyama | 107-0062 Minato-ku
Phone: +81 3 57 74 17 27
www.n-o-s.net
Subway: Omotesando
Opening hours: Mon–Sat 6 pm to 5 am, Sunday and Holiday 6 pm to 11 pm
Average price: ¥ 4000
Cuisine: International

Nylon

Design: RIC DESIGN

B2F, Caretta Shiodome Bldg., 1-8-2 Higashi-Shinbasi | 105-7090 Minato-ku
Phone: +81 3 55 37 56 46
www.create-restaurants.co.jp
Subway: Shiodome
Opening hours: Mon–Thu 11:30 am to 11:30 pm,
Fri–Sat and Holiday 11 am to 11:30 pm
Menu price: Lunch ¥ 1000, Dinner ¥ 4000
Cuisine: Mediterranean

Olives

Design: David Rockwell Group | Chef: Todd English

5F, West Walk, Roppongi Hills, 6-10-1 Roppongi | 106-0032 Minato-ku
Phone: +81 3 54 13 95 71
www.soho-s.co.jp/olives/hills_fs.html
Subway: Roppongi
Opening hours: Every day 11 am to 3:30 pm, 5:30 to 11:30 pm
Menu price: Lunch ¥ 2500, Dinner ¥ 10000
Cuisine: Modern Mediterranean

Oto Oto

Design: Hashimoto Yukio Design Studio Inc.
Grand chef: Masayuki Nakano | Main chef: Yasushi Ookura

Bekkan Shinjuku Center Bldg., 1-25-1 Nishishinjuku | 163-0690 Shinjuku-ku
Phone: +81 3 59 08 22 82
www.otooto.jp
Subway: Shinjuku
Opening hours: Every day 11:30 am to 11:30 pm
Menu price: Lunch ¥ 1200, Dinner ¥ 4500
Cuisine: Japanese

The Dining

Design: Terry McGinnity, Kanko Kikaku Sekkei Sha Co. Ltd.
Chef: Haruhisa Noguchi

26-32 Fl, Shinagawa East One Tower, 2-16-1 Konan | 108-8282 Minato-ku
Phone: +81 3 45 62 15 81
www.stringshotel.com/restaurants/dng
Subway: Shinagawa
Opening hours: Mon–Fri 6:30 am to 12 midnight,
Sat, Sun and Holiday 6:30 am to 11:30 pm
Menu price: Lunch ¥ 3500
Cuisine: French fusion cuisine

Filet of Sole "Venetian Style"

Seezungenfilet nach venezianischer Art
Filet de sole à la Vénitienne
Filete de lenguado a la veneciana
Filetto di sogliola alla veneziana

4 sole filets
2 tbsp butter
Vegetable stock
2 firm tomatoes
1 fennel
2 gloves garlic
Salt, pepper
2 twigs tarragon
1 tbsp tomato paste
2 tbsp olive oil
9 oz Basmati risotto as side dish

Cut filets in half lengthwise. Grease four metal rings with butter and line with two filet strips. Steam in a pot with some vegetable stock. Skin tomatoes, quarter, remove seeds. Strain seeds through a sieve and put juice aside. Mince fennel and garlic and roast them in a pan. Add set aside tomato juice. Season tomato flesh shells, put in a baking dish, top with fennel-garlic mix and tarragon twigs and bake for 30 minutes in a 320 °F oven.
In the meantime cook Basmati risotto.
Take the tomatoes out of the fond, strain liquid. Set aside.
Get the rings off the filets and fill them to 1/3 with tomato shells. Top with Basmati risotto.
For the sauce heat tomato fond and season with tomato paste, minced tarragon and olive oil.
Place sole rings in the middle of the plates and pour sauce around them.

4 Seezungenfilets
2 EL Butter
Gemüsebrühe
2 festfleischige Tomaten
1 Fenchelknolle
2 Knoblauchzehen
Salz, Pfeffer
2 Zweige Estragon
1 EL Tomatenmark
2 EL Olivenöl
250 g Basmati Risotto als Beilage

Die Filets der Länge nach halbieren. Vier Metallringe mit Butter einfetten und mit je zwei Filetstreifen auslegen. In einem Topf mit etwas Gemüsebrühe gar dämpfen.
Tomaten häuten, vierteln, Kerne entfernen. Die Kerne durch ein Sieb streichen und den Saft auffangen. Den Fenchel und Knoblauch fein hacken, in einer Pfanne anbraten und mit dem Tomatensaft ablöschen. Die Tomatenfilets würzen, in eine Form geben, mit dem Fenchel-Knoblauch-Mix übergießen und mit Estragonzweigen bedecken. Im Ofen bei 160 °C ca. 30 Minuten garen.
In der Zwischenzeit das Basmati-Risotto kochen. Die Tomaten aus dem Sud nehmen, die Flüssigkeit durch ein Sieb gießen. Aufbewahren. Die Filets aus den Ringen lösen und zu 1/3 mit den Tomaten füllen. Basmati-Risotto daraufgeben.
Für die Sauce den Sud erhitzen und mit Tomatenmark, gehacktem Estragon und Olivenöl abschmecken. Seezungenringe in der Mitte des Tellers anrichten und mit der Sauce umgießen.

4 filets de sole
2 c. à soupe de beurre
Bouillon de légumes
2 tomates à la chair ferme
1 bulbe de fenouil
2 gousses d'ail
Sel, poivre
2 branches d'estragon
1 c. à soupe de concentré de tomates
2 c. à soupe d'huile d'olive
250 g de riz Basmati

Coupez les filets en deux dans le sens de la longueur. Enduisez de beurre quatre cercles métalliques et garnissez-les chacun de deux morceaux de filet. Cuisez-les à l'étuvée dans une casserole avec un peu de bouillon de légumes. Pelez et coupez les tomates en quatre, épépinezles. Passez les pépins au chinois et recueillez le jus. Hachez finement le fenouil et l'ail, cuisez-les à la poêle et mouillez avec le jus de tomate. Assaisonnez à votre goût les morceaux de tomate, mettez-les dans un moule, versez le mélange fenouil-ail par dessus et couvrez de branches d'estragon. Faites cuire au four à 160 °C pendant 30 minutes environ.
Entre-temps, faites cuire le riz Basmati.
Retirez les tomates de la décoction, passez le liquide au chinois. Réservez.
Enlevez les filets des cercles et remplissez-les au tiers de tomates. Ajoutez ensuite le riz Basmati par-dessus.
Pour la sauce, chauffez la décoction, assaisonnez à votre goût avec le concentré de tomates, l'estragon haché et l'huile d'olive. Disposez les filets de sole au centre d'une assiette et versez la sauce par-dessus

---

4 filetes de lenguado
2 cucharadas de mantequilla
Caldo de verdura
2 tomates carnosos
1 bulbo de hinojo
2 dientes de ajo
Sal, pimienta
2 ramas de estragón
1 cucharada de concentrado de tomate
2 cucharadas de aceite de oliva
250 g de arroz basmati

Cortar los filetes por la mitad longitudinalmente. Engrasar con mantequilla cuatro aros de metal y colocar encima de cada uno dos tiras de filete. Cocer al vapor en un cazo con un poco de caldo de verdura.
Pelar los tomates, cortarlos en cuartos, quitar las pepitas. Pasar por un colador las pepitas y reservar el jugo. Picar finamente el hinojo y el ajo, dorar en una sartén y verter el jugo de tomate. Condimentar los gajos de tomate, introducir en un molde, rociar con la mezcla de hinojo y ajo y cubrir con los tallos de estragón. Cocinar en el horno a 160 °C durante aprox. 30 minutos.
Entretanto cocer el arroz basmati.
Retirar los tomates del caldo y colar el líquido con colador. Reservar.
Separar los filetes de los aros y rellenar con los tomates hasta un tercio. Añadir por encima el arroz basmati.
Para la salsa calentar el caldo y aderezar con concentrado de tomate, estragón picado y aceite de oliva al gusto. Colocar los anillos de lenguado en el centro del plato y rociar con la salsa

---

4 filetti di sogliola
2 cucchiai di burro
Brodo di verdure
2 pomodori con polpa soda
1 finocchio
2 spicchi d'aglio
Sale, pepe
2 rametti di dragoncello
1 cucchiai di concentrato di pomodoro
2 cucchiai d'olio d'oliva
250 g di riso basmati

Tagliare i filetti a metà per il lungo. Imburrare quattro anelli di metallo e stendervi in ciascuno due filetti. Cuocere a vapore in una pentola con un po' di brodo di verdure.
Privare i pomodori della pelle e dei semi e tagliarli in quarti. Passare la polpa al setaccio raccogliendo l'acqua di vegetazione. Soffriggere in una padella il finocchio e l'aglio ben tritati e bagnare con l'acqua del pomodoro. Insaporire i filetti al pomodoro, metterli in un tegame, cospargerli col il miscuglio di finocchio e aglio e coprire con gambi di dragoncello. Mettere in forno a circa 160 °C, e lasciare cuocere per ca. 30 minuti.
Nel frattempo fare cuocere il risotto basmati.
Togliere i pomodori dal decotto, passare al setaccio il liquido e conservarlo.
Togliere i filetti dagli anelli e farcirli a un terzo con i pomodori. Sopra a questi stendere il risotto basmati.
Per fare la salsa riscaldate il decotto e condite con concentrato di pomodoro, dragoncello tritato e olio d'oliva. Disponete gli anelli di sogliola al centro del piatto e circondateli di salsa.

Zipang

Design: Takashi Sugimoto

14F, Nagatacho, 2-14-3 Akasaka Excel Hotel Tokyu | 100-0014 Chiyoda-ku
Phone: +81 3 35 80 36 61
zipang@nadaman.co.jp
Subway: Akasaka-Mitsuke
Opening hours: Every day 5 pm to 3 am
Average price: ¥ 8000
Cuisine: Stylish Japanese

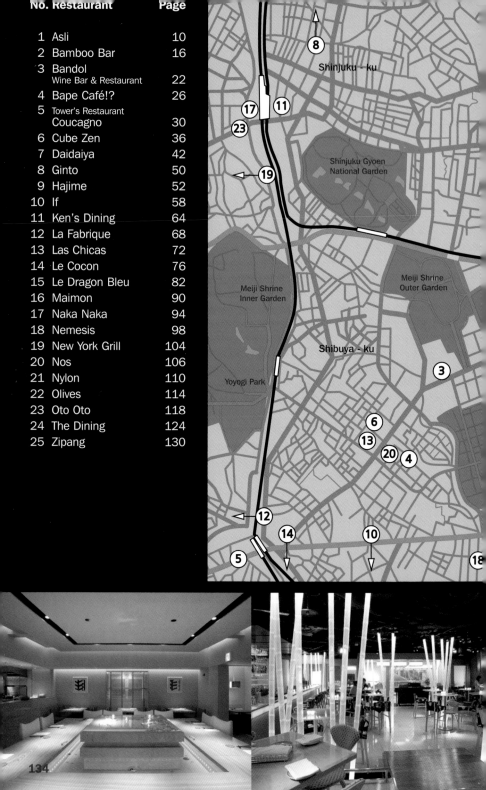

Shinjuku - ku

Shinjuku Gyoen National Garden

Meiji Shrine Outer Garden

Meiji Shrine Inner Garden

Shibuya - ku

Yoyogi Park

134

Chiyoda - ku

Imperial Palace

Marunouchi

① 1

㉕ 25

Hibiya Park

⑮ 15

⑨ 9

Minato - ku

⑦ 7

② 2 ㉒ 22

㉑ 21

⑯ 16

㉔ 24

Cool Restaurants

Size: 14 x 21.5 cm / 5 1/2 x 8 in.
136 pp
Flexicover

c. 130 color photographs
Text in English, German, French,
Spanish and (*) Italian

Other titles in the same series:

Amsterdam (*)
ISBN 3-8238-4588-8

Barcelona (*)
ISBN 3-8238-4586-1

Berlin (*)
ISBN 3-8238-4585-3

Hamburg (*)
ISBN 3-8238-4599-3

London
ISBN 3-8238-4568-3

Los Angeles (*)
ISBN 3-8238-4589-6

Milan (*)
ISBN 3-8238-4587-X

New York
ISBN 3-8238-4571-3

Paris
ISBN 3-8238-4570-5

To be published in the
same series:

Brussels	Munich
Chicago	Rome
Geneva	Stockholm
Madrid	Sydney
Miami	Vienna
Moscow	Zurich

teNeues